The Scholarship Thief
Undergrad Edition

Dedication

*for my nephews Semajhe and
Roger Netherly
–go for your dreams!*

Orangia Lemle
*You taught me the importance of education
when the road was difficult.*

Orangia Lemle was one of the first people who believed in my education when I felt it was impossible. Through the *Young Saint's* program at Faithway Missionary Baptist Church in Los Angeles, California, she celebrated graduates for their success by having a ceremony, and more than often, instilled in me the desire to never quit. She nurtured my desire to go to school, and supported me behind the scenes. The long phone conversations, and seed planting you instilled in my life has brought me to this point. May you continue to R.I.P. knowing that the work you have done for students will forever continue.

"It must be borne in mind that the
tragedy of life does not lie in not reaching your goal.
The tragedy of life lies in having no goal to reach."

–Benjamin E. Mays

Praise and Encouragement for *The Scholarship Thief*

Never limit your possibilities. The benefits of pursuing higher learning, of any kind, are endless both personally and professionally. Although many are very bright and qualified for such pursuits, they are frequently unaware of the countless possibilities available to them. The right information can change the course of your life and how you view perceived obstacles. It definitely changed mine. Find your passion and find a way to fund it, the opportunities are endless.

Angelia M. Baxter – Bachelors of Business Administration Management

Congratulations on picking up this book! It is an excellent first step in your pursuit of higher education. Please know there will always be a scholarship that you qualify for. Focus on that and that alone and you will be well on your way to having an educational experience that is centered on learning versus finances.

Marcita Enis – Bachelors of Art in Print Journalism, San Francisco State University

The Scholarship Thief will change the way you view education and scholarships. It is a brief collection of encouragement, essays, tips and resources prepared to help you succeed. It is a contribution to those who are searching for the help, and a guide to help propel you forward.

Toi Nichelle – Bachelors of Arts, English: Creative Writing. CEO/Founder The Scholarship Thief Foundation and Dream Loud Ink, Publishing

This book will bring you such knowledge that you too will be able to attend school with little to no debt. This information she gives should be given in all high schools, and even junior high schools. Take notice and expand your horizon.

Helen Gill-Smith –Bachelors of Arts degree in Business Management

AMAZING! I'm in complete awe of Toi Nichelle right now. She's an amazing author and writes a fresh, intelligently written, educational, innovative, and informative book that I could not get enough of. I found it really enjoyable to read. I'm glad that our society is finally making place for books like this to exist. This book is like the guide-to-securing your academic future, only much better! Each one of us has something to offer and we have a responsibility to ourselves to discover what that is. That's the opportunity an education can provide. Education is a life-long process that needs to be reinforced through life. Without education, life can be disastrous and detrimental. I wholeheartedly recommend this book to anyone who wants to attend college and is serious about their education and career. Ben Franklin said it best when he wrote, "An investment in knowledge pays the best interest."

Tammy Doss –Executive Officer, The Scholarship Thief Foundation & Advocate for Education

"I want for nothing. Everything in my life pre-destined have already made its way to me –I'm just walking into it. I desire great things, and so shall they come to me. Whatever I speak shall be, so I acknowledge the good things. I am aware that my very being is a manifestation of grace and mercy. I am more than what you see, really, I am more than what you see."

Toi Nichelle

Also
by
Toi Nichelle

The Hush Language
Mirror to my Soul

The Scholarship Thief
Undergrad Edition

Copyright © 2016
Toi Nichelle
All rights reserved

No part of this book may be reproduced in any form, except for the inclusion of brief quotations in a literary review, without permission in writing from the author or publisher. The support of the author's rights is appreciated.

All quotes in this book are original material of the author, unless otherwise noted, and should not be used without permission.

Essays used are property of the author. Recommendation letters used with permission.

ISBN 10: 09786817-6-2
ISBN 13: 978-0-9786817-6-0

Published by Dream Loud Ink, Publishing
Typeset & Editing by: Dream Loud Ink Publishing
Email : dreamloudinc@yahoo.com

Co-Editor –Tammy Doss

Disclaimer

This book is meant to be a useful aid of encouragement and motivation. No form of this book, including sample essays and letters are to be copied and pasted. Plagiarism is against the law.

I am in no way proclaiming to be an expert, therefore, the information you see in this book is a mere contribution to help students during their process. It is not to be taken as exact and accurate, as academic information changes per year. Please, as you read this book, use what is helpful and research on your own for other information you may need.

Special thanks to these supporters

Anna McCoy –W.A.N. (Woman Act Now)
Claudia Acevedo –Scholarship Office –Los Medanos College
David Wick –Study Abroad Office –SF State
Tammy Doss –Advocate for Education, Los Angeles, California

Professors who have written Recommendation Letters

Dana Teen Lomax –Professor of Creative Arts, SF State
Elise Ficarra –Poetry Center Support Coordinator, SF State
Steve Dickison –Professor of Creative Arts, SF State
Brian Thorstenson –Professor of Creative Arts, SF State
Lauren V. Jarvis –Professor of African History, SF State
Reginald Turner –Career Center, Los Medanos College
Laura Subia –EOPS, Los Medanos College
Barbara Austin –Professor of Creative Arts, Los Medanos College
Donald Kaiper –Professor of History, Los Medanos College

Those who have submitted essays, encouraging words and motivation

Helen Gill- Smith
Angelia Baxter
Marcita Enis
Emily Daniella Brown
Lori D. Taylor
Jalea Harris
Darice Ingram
Shantelle Ortiz
Rashauna R. Smallwood
Tara Powell

Table of Contents

The Desire

What is the Scholarship Thief? - 1
Forward: My Story -2
The Desire Exercise - 6
Motivation Corner –Helen Gill-Smith - 11
Action takes Courage - 14
Motivation Corner –Lori D. Taylor - 16

The Search

How to begin? What to look for? - 19
Estimated Tuition Breakdown - 22
Blank Table –Tuition - 24
Motivation Corner –Jalea Nicole Harris - 25
Living Cost – 27
Blank Table –Fees - 30
Financial Aid –Using it wisely - 31
Personal Motivation - 33
Motivation Corner –Shantelle Ortiz - 35

The Process

Personal Goals Table - 39
How to write an essay - 40
Sample Scholarship Essays 44-53
Sample Sponsorship Cover Letter -56
Actual Letter -57
Sample Scholarship Sheet - 60

Motivation Corner –Darice A. Ingram - 61
Scholarship Fact Sheet - 63
The Interview Process - 65
Motivation Corner –Emily Daniella Brown - 68
The Importance of Mentors - 70
Handling Rejection - 73
Sample Recommendation Letters - 76
Motivation Corner –Rashauna R. Smallwood - 91
Thank You Letters - 94
Studying Abroad? – 98

The Result

Motivation Corner –Tara Powell - 115
Additional Tips -117
Last minute Check List -121
Congratulations -122

Starter Essay Questions -124
FAQ'S Answered -125
Author's Bio -127
Scholarship Resource Alphabetical Listing -129
Contact Info - 138

The Scholarship Thief

This book is about change. I have realized that however you perceive change is the same way it will manifest. Education can be tough when you have certain obstacles standing in your way. This book is about learning how to see yourself beyond the circumstance because no matter how hard it may seem, it can happen. The title of this book *The Scholarship Thief* is about positioning yourself to receive what is rightfully yours. This book represents using your financial resources wisely, and learning to use the scholarship for your education and not personal desires. Despite all the misconceptions of applying for scholarships, it all starts in your mind. Do not cheat yourself of an education because you choose not to get involved. You must do the work, write the essay, attend workshops, go to interviews, and speak with your professors if you want to see change manifest. The more you procrastinate, the further you will remain from walking the stage.

The truth is that college not only allows you to obtain a degree, but college, whether community or university, will provide three things: people, communication, and trust skills, which I had none of these. Let's face it. In today's world, you are going to need to know how to deal with people whether on the job or in the grocery store; communicate effectively with supervisors, peers and friends; and trust your ability and others to get the job done.

With the skills above, you will have been taught to be a well-rounded, diverse human being ready to challenge your place in the world. If it is your desire to complete your education and you need information from someone who went through the process, stopped the process and started again, then keep reading.

Forward: My Story

Have you ever felt there was more you needed to do in life? The world constantly moved while it felt as if your life was playing the balancing act just trying to keep up. You finally get to a point where you realize that life will not stop for you, and you have to make some decisions on how to make the best of what you have been dealt with. Personally, I know this feeling well. After dealing with so many circumstances and challenges in life, I began to feel drained. There was always this constant downfall of wanting to do better, but never getting to the point where I could actually do what I knew I needed to. Amongst other abilities, education was my way to starting the process of change. Briefly, I would like to share some of my challenges I experienced down the academic path of change, while also sharing the ways I encouraged myself to keep it moving no matter what.

I first started college after my senior year of high school in 2001. Because of personal problems I faced at home with being homeless, abused and often teased my academics started to suffer. Let me just make something clear –I was always one of the smartest students in my class as a child, attending highly accredited schools with honor achievement. I fell in love with words at a young age, worked hard in school where I kept straight *A's* and challenged myself to go above and beyond in the classroom. This all happened before the age of ten, and while most children were out playing carefree, I was hidden somewhere reading. I remember when I had an orientation at a school where I would be attending my first grade year. It was a highly motivated catholic school, so of course there were strict nuns who watched every student like a hawk. During this brief meeting, they had me draw a family with a house because they wanted to test my ability to see and do beyond what I was told. A few stick figures, a somewhat round sun –the best that a first grader could do, right? Well, this was not the case because when the nun looked down at my paper I had drawn a 3D picture of what they expected to see as stick figures. I gave them clothes and shoes, drew a fence around the house and made the sun distant in the sky with the birds soaring in circles. The nun called my mom and other nuns to see my drawing, and I overheard them say, "The little one here is gifted." While this may be farfetched from being highly gifted, I did understand that I wanted to always be better, and do more.

Growing up, I experienced painful situations at home that forced me to become an adult at an early age. While a lot of abuse was taking place I continued to grow up. I became more silent in my communication, and although I desired to do better, I allowed my academics to suffer. The *A's* I once had dropped tremendously, and I stopped caring altogether.

Truthfully, this is a book all in itself, so let us fast forward to my senior year of high school. I had still made my way into the magnet program, which was designed for the 'smart kids'. Even in this program, I fought to graduate. I walked the stage, got my diploma, and with no guidance, I enrolled myself into Trade Technical College in Los Angeles, California. Those same habits followed me in my first year of college, and my academics suffered greatly. It came to a point where I needed to work full-time in order to survive, and because I was under twenty-five years of age with no one to claim me because I had been taking care of myself since I was a child, I had to drop out. Of course, when you do not have any guidance, you are liable to do things the wrong way. I dropped out of college, not understanding that I had to physically drop my classes. This was not told to me early on, so I just stopped showing up to class, not realizing that I was still considered an 'active' student. While some of the teachers dropped me after I did not show up, others kept me on the roster and gave me a failing grade, which ended up on my transcripts. This went on for a few years, and soon it caught up with me. I would re-enroll into another college and/or class, stop showing up when I had to work, and it affected my grades. Eventually, I saw the pattern and wanted to make a drastic change. I moved around a lot, but soon settled in East Bay, California. In 2008, I made it up in my mind that I wanted to finish what I started, and stick with it no matter what. When I decided this, I had to request my transcripts from ALL the previous colleges attended, which came to about five. My cumulative GPA was low, and all of the failing grades, and withdrawals haunted me. *Surely, this would not work out in my favor,* I thought. I made an appointment with the academic advisors at Los Medanos Community College, and they were shocked. I felt at odds, and wanted to give up my desire to obtain my Associate's degree, but I stuck with it.

In May 2011, I graduated from Los Medanos Community College with my A.A. degree in Liberal Arts and Humanities, and three scholarships that would follow me to San Francisco State University upon transfer. I was also asked to be a speaker at the scholarship banquet, and a visiting speaker at the college's annual scholarship workshop. I was also nominated to be the keynote speaker for the graduation ceremony by the academic staff. Although I was not the chosen speaker, the staff assured me that I had completely changed my academic path and made life more possible to live. I transferred to San Francisco State University in fall 2011, and had an opportunity to study abroad in the United Kingdom for one academic year at the University of East Anglia. Things can work in your favor, even if your past academic history is not that great. Upon traveling to Norwich, England, where I would settle for a year, I was financially protected with scholarships that paid my tuition, residence accommodations, flight transportation, ground transportation for the year I was there, all my traveling needs, food etc. I even had the privilege to back-pack throughout Europe to places like, Amsterdam, Paris and Venice, Italy. I came back to the United States debt free of student loans, with an experience that will last a lifetime. A little over a week later, I graduated from San Francisco State University with my B.A. degree in English: Creative Writing.

This is the sum of my academic background in a nutshell, so if there are certain challenges that you may be facing, DO NOT GIVE UP. I am a mere testimony of what can happen to someone, even when it seems like all doors are closed. There may be times you feel that your grades are not good enough –that's okay. Keep trying, do better the next time and go for your dreams, academic and beyond.

In this book, I have included tips, financial breakdowns, sample essays, facts you should consider when planning out your year, and some resources that have helped me along the way. You will not regret reading this book because I have shared with you the information that really helped me throughout my years of undergrad. For your convenience, I have also divided this book into four sections: the desire, the search, the process, the result. If there is more information you may need, or encouragement during this process, email me at: dreamloudinc@yahoo.com.

THE DESIRE

"You would have never been chosen, if you did not have inside of you the will to do it."

What do you desire to do in life? What are your goals and dreams? What are you pursuing right now, and what do you need to help make it easier? What is your focus on at this point? Are you keeping a steady pace in the pursuit of your journey? Or are you allowing life's obstacles to keep you on one level?

I asked myself all of these questions during my journey to higher education, and truthfully, I still do. It is very important that you continue to speak to yourself. Speak all that is positive, asking those questions which will allow you to set foot down the path of your desires. Let's take a minute and focus on some of the above questions with an exercise.

Q. What do you desire to do in life?

A. I desire to be a writer, pursue higher education, and be mentor to youth who are faced with academic and personal disadvantages.

Q. What are you pursuing right now?

A. I am pursuing higher career goals in the field of professional writing, as well as seeking opportunities in the school system as a motivational speaker and youth advocate for education.

Now you try:

Q. What do you desire to do in life?

A. _____
_____
_____

Q. What is your focus on at this point?

A. _____
_____
_____

Q. What do you need to help you?

A. _____
_____
_____

I have learned that you have to begin writing down what you want out of life. Make changes along the way as necessary, and when you accomplish that which you have declared on paper, just keep going. The key here is to never allow circumstances in life to hold you back from your desires. I believe that when you are enrolling in school to pursue your degree, you need to really know what field you want to study in at some point, and how you wish to apply it to your career goals upon graduation. It is okay in the beginning if you are unsure of the field you wish to study; this is why there are counselors to help guide you along the way.

A degree is more than a piece of paper. It is clearly a pledge of honor that says you have dedicated yourself wholeheartedly to something until it was complete. You endured class lectures, study groups, class presentations, professor/student meetings, random unannounced quizzes, midterms, final tests, essays, dissertations, being tired and having to work a job, but still pushing through. By all means, completing your degree says that you are full of accomplishment, and you do not know what the word *quit* means. When I think of having a desire to do something in life, there are many words that come to mind. Here are a few that I automatically think of:

- ✓ Passion
- ✓ Fearlessness
- ✓ Accountability
- ✓ Determination
- ✓ Finishing
- ✓ Release
- ✓ Opportunity
- ✓ Aspire

All of these words scream desire to me. I want to take a moment to look at each word, and define it based on my perception first, then giving you, the reader, a chance to do the same. If you're paying attention, you'll notice that in the beginning of the book, I noted that change is the way you perceive it. This is what these words are about. How are you perceiving yourself and dreams in the word *desire*?

1. Passion –The type of feeling that causes you to lose sleep at night because your every thought is consumed by it.

2. Fearlessness –Learning how to not be afraid of what you desire, even when obstacle has a pillow on the left side of your bed.

3. Accountability –Holding yourself to your dreams, like shackles to a prisoner.

4. <u>Determination</u> –No matter what happens during the course of your journey, you fight with both fists, and walk with both feet.

5. <u>Finishing</u> –Seeing the end result before you make it, and using it as fuel to quicken your pace.

6. <u>Release</u> –Allowing all of the fight inside of you to pull through, while letting go of the dead weight that is hindering you.

7. <u>Opportunity</u> –Welcoming change to show itself, and greeting challenge with an "I got this" mentality.

8. <u>Aspire</u> –Speaking your success, while encouraging yourself in the midst of what you're hoping for.

Exercise

Are there any words that come to your mind when you think of the word desire? Use the space below to help you define your thoughts, while seeing where you are in the process. Take your time, there is no rush here.

1. _____

2. _____

3. _____

4. _____

5. _____

6. _____

7. _____

Having the desire to pursue higher education is a great desire to have. Do not get sidetracked by what you physically see because sometimes you will have to find the courage to look beyond it.

Helpful Tip:

Desires change as you change.
Try writing down your thoughts in a separate journal.
This will help you to keep track of how you feel about something, and if your desire for it is still there.

Motivation Corner

Never too late

My name is Helen Gill-Smith. In 2011 I received my B.A. degree in Business Management at the ripe age of 46. Bless the Lord. It was a long journey to get there due to struggles and decisions of my own in my life. It seemed like every time I would try to go to college and get ahead, something dramatic would happen just when I got started. I was blessed to graduate from high school early and attend college, which they allowed me the pleasure to graduate on stage with my class. During my first year I became pregnant, and although it was a joy, I was met with many medical issues which caused me to drop out. Upon my return I was faced with a bill instead of a scholarship, causing me to have no more fight within me, so I went to work caring for my child as a single mother.

As the years went on I was married, divorced, and soon birthed another child, then married again. In between time I tried again to attend college and complete what I had started, but with my constant medical issues and struggles raising a family with no help, it did not happen. By the time my children were in their late teens, I was ready to go back to college determined to complete my A.A. degree no matter what.

By this time I was able to attend online classes, enrolled as a full-time student, and well capable of working a computer and meeting deadlines. The one thing that challenged me was learning how to research and prepare myself for the constant test-taking curriculum that was provided. This brought me back into the reality of school, especially on a college level. *What a shocker!* But the end result was great joy.

To all my fellow college students young and seasoned –you can find so much joy in completion and accomplishment. You'll not only gain a world of knowledge, but a world of friends along the way. Even if they are online students or teachers. Through online, the world is yours.

While working and going to school I was able to advance on my job from a lead clerk to a supervisor, and in a position to assist management in many different areas of the job. My degree has opened doors I had not even thought of. I knew what I wanted, but God had another plan. Although I am not a manager, yet, I am working with managers and leaders across the board –from a city job to numerous nonprofit organizations, as well as churches and Facebook as administrator, including Office Manager, Secretary, and Overseer of a music company. Yes I keep myself busy.

At this point in my life and those that I work for I am not looking for a big payout, because it is all about what I enjoy doing and who I enjoy working for and with. At any time I can quit my job and retire and just work for all of these organizations, but I choose – get it – *I choose* to stay and continue to work. I am in a position where I do not have to work, but I want to work my eight hours a day.

In a year or so, I plan to leave this job and work in management, however, if God leads me to work more for these nonprofit organizations, which I believe he will, then so it shall be. If you enjoy and love what you do, no amount of money can replace that. With a degree, it comes easier to do because there is no struggle as to how it should be done. Without my degree, learning, researching, and all the training, I would not be able to handle this load or the work.

My encouragement is for you to continue to grow, learn, reach, stretch, and pursue your dreams, ambitions, degrees, and your heart's desire. The world is an open book, however in this world; we need training and degrees to make it in many places. Not having a degree can hold you down, back, and to a level that you feel defeated and beneath everyone else.

Never give up on your dreams. Never give in to the pressures of life. Go for it. Take the plunge. With all that stood in my way, I pressed on because I was determined and knew I would be filled with joy unlike any other when it comes to education. It is so important to life itself because I truly believe that *knowledge is power*, and because I do, it is engraved in my high school ring. That is how long I have believed in those words.

This book will bring you such knowledge that you too will be able to attend school with little to no debt. Take notice and expand your horizon. I have supported Toi for the few years I have known her, and it was a joy to watch her grow and experience the world through learning. If she can do it, you can too. This information she gives should be given in all high schools, and even junior high schools. Why? Because Knowledge is Power!

Helen Gill-Smith is a mother, friend, songstress and mentor to many. She has received her Bachelors of Arts degree in Business Administration. She currently resides in East Bay, California with her loving family.

Action takes *Courage*

Did you know that there are thousands upon thousands of individuals stuck on their decision to go to college? Many of which take out loans but never finish their program? There are many statistics to show this, but this book is not designed to provide statistics. This book is designed for encouragement and resources so that students, teen and older, will have the support to stay in the race, and finish strong. If you want statistics instead, try your local library, but if you want to hear the stories of others, this book is for you. Action takes courage, and you've proven that by picking up this book. Let's begin.

If you are still in high school, or wanting to attend college for the first time, you need to make sure that you have a plan of action. To start off this book, it is important to get you in the right mind frame to begin this process. Let's take a look at a few things you should do before you begin applying.

1. Have you searched out the school of your choice? If not, why? This is the most important step in the process. Go to the university's website so that you can learn about your department program and selection process. Most major departments have different steps when applying. This is why it is important to check because you do not want to miss a step that will disqualify you from your program. Determine that you will start now if you have not searched out the college/university you are interested in.
2. Think about what sets you apart now because there are a great number of applicants going for the same program and/or scholarship. You do not want to be one of the ones to not get an acceptance letter.
3. Determine how much of your personal finances will be used to fund your education. There will be a section on the FAFSA and scholarship forms that will ask this question. You want to make sure that you are aware of the amount of money you can pay out of pocket, and how much you need.
4. What is the length of your program? How long will it take you to complete your degree and graduate? Most scholarship

applications will ask you to list your expected graduation date. It is important to know the year you will graduate so that you can begin to develop a plan on the load you can carry on a semester basis.
5. Have you made a special visit to the college campus? Taking a trip to the campus will not only give you an opportunity to tour the grounds, but it will allow you to visit their scholarship office to see what additional funding may be available to you. It is also your chance to make connections with students and faculty.

It is okay if you do not know everything. When I first started, I had to learn what to do, and it took me some time. Even then, I am still learning every day what I can do to make it easier for myself, and others. Do not overwhelm yourself with what you do not know. Instead, ask as many questions as you can to help you.

Motivation Corner

Favor and Redemption

It has been said, "Time waits for no one", but I feel like it did. Time was on my side. Believe it or not, it is on your side, too. There is always time to go back to school and pursue your dreams and achieve success in your life. Never give up. Here I am 50 years old, and finishing my Doctorate of Ministry degree at San Francisco Theological Seminary, San Anselmo California.

In 1983, I graduated from high school. With no real direction for my life, I didn't take advantage of the opportunities presented to me. Every morning my friend and I got up, ready to head off to school at the local junior college in our town. We would get as far as the parking lot after smoking weed, and we would sit there deciding to leave shortly after. I don't know what we were thinking at the time, but the inevitable happened. We dropped out.

I didn't realized just how important an education really is, especially in this day and time. It's hard with one, so think how hard it would be without it. Having your education allows you to market yourself better in pursuit of great career opportunities. Many job seekers, some who have years of experience, may not even be considered for a job, or they may be passed over for a candidate who has a degree, or more education, but less experience.

It has been a tough journey, but 7 years after I graduated, I started realizing how important education really is after feeling like I was in prison. During this time of transition, I bought a new car because it was what I needed. In order for me to maintain the note and up keep on my brand new car, I had to work. Often, I found myself saying, "If I did not have this car, I would be back in school full-time. *"No matter how much you want to complete your goals in life, there is always your thinking that stops you."*

On February 6, 1989 –on my father's birthday, I had a car accident. My car flipped over twice. I just knew I was going to die. Mentally and emotionally I felt great because I believed I was given another opportunity and outlook on life. I was at a point where anything and everyone who was a negative force in hindering me from pursuing a fulfilling life was being removed. I say this because before the accident I was living a life of crime. I worked at a major department store, Capwells in Livingston California, where I stole people's credit cards and charged thousands of dollars in merchandise. As soon as I got out of my car, in a daze I thought about all the wrong I had been doing and all that I thought I was getting away with, but almost paid with my life. I was emotionally and mentally full of gratitude and sorrow for all that I had done to people. This is when I realized even more that we don't ever get away with wrong in our lives. It pays to be right.

Although my car was completely totaled out, I walked away from the accident unharmed. There was not a scratch anywhere. The insurance company eventually paid me for my car. With another $13,000 in my pocket, I thought about buying me another car. Suddenly, my own words flooded my mind, *if I did not have this car, I would be back in school full-time.* In the stillness of the moment a question came to me, "Do you want another car or do you want your education?" Immediately, I knew that I wanted an education. Reasoning within myself, I said, "I will get my education so that I can get the kind of car I desire in the long run. The car can wait." What I learned is that life will always place us before doors of opportunity; the question is –which one would we be inclined to take? For me, I chose to follow the road of learning. Understand that education today is a luxury.

Don't let oppositions deter you. I always say, "The greater the sacrifice the greater the reward." Although I had many oppositions and challenges, I never lost hope or my focus. Stay focused; stay the course! You might believe you lack the finances, confidence and support, but never be discourage or deterred. There might be moments when you won't know whether to throw the towel in or out. If ever in doubt, be still and do nothing. Again, stay the course and press towards your goal and never lose heart. "Keep Your Eye's on The Prize!"

I had to do just that –keep my eyes on the prize. After going back to school, I eventually graduated 6 years later with two Associate of Arts degrees, a Bachelors of Arts degree in Sociology with a minor in Social Work, and a Master's of Divinity Degree in Theology. Currently, I am finishing up my doctoral pursuit at San Francisco Theological Seminary even though my expected graduation date of May 2008 is long past.

Years had gone by and I was feeling bad because if I start something, I do not like to stop until it is finished. This was the one thing that was incomplete in my life. One day a friend asked if I was going back to school to finish. I told her no. I couldn't even wrap my mind around school at the time. I was not interested in a title or another degree. A week later while at church, my Bishop, Christopher Carl Smith was generally speaking to the congregation. He said, "Go back and pick God up where you laid God down and complete that which" he shouts, "YOU", he stops right in front of me as he was talking, "KNOW IS INCOMPLETE IN YOUR LIFE!" I thought about my recent conversation with my friend. First thing Monday morning, I called the seminary and left a detail message for the registrar. Three days later she called me with so much excitement to tell me the Board of Trustees had just concluded their meeting and approved me to come back and complete the program that I was told was my last opportunity in 2009. Although it has been said, "time waits on no one", time not only waited, it is on my side! Always remember the greater the sacrifice the greater the reward!

Lori D. Taylor received her two Associate degrees in social sciences and general education, her Bachelors of Arts in Sociology and Masters of Divinity in Theology. She currently lives in Oakland, California where is completing her Doctorate to pursue ministry in the area of specialized pastoral counseling, and teaching.

THE SEARCH

"If you are constantly searching for ways to reach for your dream but are feeling stuck and overwhelmed wanting to quit, try thinking of how your life will be without purpose. Still want to quit?"

I define the search as an opportunity for you to begin looking at what is available to you. There is no obligation or deadline in searching for information, so take your time when looking, but start early. Do not overwhelm yourself with information. Write down what is beneficial and move on to the next. When you find the right school and scholarship that pertains to your situation, take all the information down, including deadlines, fees and possible upcoming interviews. This is where the hefty scholarship form will come in handy (see page 60 for form). You want to write down the applicable scholarship in the section provided. Applicable meaning, ONLY write down scholarships you qualify for. Begin the process of elimination. An example of this is to first look over the criteria for the scholarship. If it says something like, "100 Black Men Scholarship", and you are an Ethiopian woman, then you know that you do not qualify. Keep it moving or pass along to a friend that does. Another example of this would be to see if it is *financial need base* or an *academic scholarship*. Financial need base scholarships will often overlook low GPA or test scores and pay close attention to your needs according to the information you submitted on your FAFSA, whereas an academic scholarship will focus on a higher GPA, award recognitions and community service. If either one pertains to you, write it down, and/or pass along to a friend.

During your search, you also want to factor out your tuition cost on an academic year and semester need. List the cost of books, application fees, university fees etc. Also, leave a little breathing room, so always round up to the nearest thousand. For example, if your tuition fee for the fall semester costs $3,338 round up to $4,000. This gives you room just in case there are any unnecessary fees that creep your way.

Besides, it is always good to have a little room left over in case you get a sudden craving for coffee. This can be your best friend when sitting in a long lecture. For more information please continue reading this section, and apply what is necessary to your personal situation. In the meantime, here are a list of definitions I came up with as it regards to scholarships.

Please Note: These definitions are my own, and were written with the intent to share my understanding, and how they fit into my needs during undergrad.

1. Scholarships –a form of financial assistance given to those who have done the work, put in the time and presented themselves when opportunity came knocking. Scholarships are given with no intent of being paid back.

2. Merit Based –a form of financial assistance given to those who have reached their academic limit, and have shown exceptional work either on campus or in their community.

3. Need Based –a form of financial assistance given to those who do not necessarily have the best grades, but have consistently evolved. This scholarship is given to those with strong financial need, and may have experienced major setbacks in life, or the first to enter college in their family.

4. FAFSA – the main financial assistance program set for all students to apply and receive assistance per academic year. Before you apply for any scholarships or grants, the FAFSA MUST be complete in order to show your income. When you apply for scholarships, they will ask if you have applied, and some will ask for proof.

5. Loans –Money borrowed to advance your education, ultimately helping you to take the financial load off of your shoulders. Loans should be the last resort, if possible.

6. Grants –Financial assistance given to those who qualify, preferably high school seniors going into college for the first time. GPA will be verified and submitted, and if approved your award can vary. Like scholarships, grants are given with no intent of being paid back.

7. Sponsorships –a form of financial assistance given to those who personally seek them. Sponsorships are not always evident like scholarships, so it is up to you to inquire further and seek the right resources to obtain them. (I obtained sponsorships by writing letters to various organizations seeking assistance (see page 57).

One thing that will help you when it comes to applying for scholarships and schools is to prepare yourself. By preparing yourself, you are making sure that every area is covered before the actual deadlines have crept up on you. Preparation starts with speaking to your counselor and financial office. They may also have a board in their office with scholarship information and deadlines. Start early, seek help with your essays, apply before the deadline, and wait patiently.

Questions asked on FAFSA application:

1. Are you a U.S. citizen?
2. Are you interested in being considered for work-study?
3. What is your high school completion status?
4. What degree will you be working on?
5. What is the highest level of school completed by your parents?

Helpful Tip:

Make sure you list EVERY college or university you are considering when filling out your FAFSA, even if you do not attend. You do not want to end up going to a university you did not list, therefore making it harder for you to receive your award.

Estimated Tuition

Below, I have listed a sample estimation of tuition costs, which can be found on your student online campus account. Please be advised that all fees are different, depending on what university you attend. The fees listed in this table are not to be taken as exact, and are merely to be used as an example to assist you in your financial planning.

Per semester

Invoice Date	Description	Min. Due	Total Owed
17-Jul-12	Tuition Fee Fall	X	2,985.00
17-Jul-12	Student Body	X	80.00
17-Jul-12	Recreation Fall	X	100.00
17-Jul-12	Campus Health Services	X	150.00
17 Jul-12	Athletics	X	70.00
17-Jul-12	Campus Services Card		5.00
17-Jul-12	Other	X	

Total: 3,390.00

Please note:

This table should help you to better understand the breakdown of student fees, and what you as a student are accountable for. Most colleges and universities will charge for the above fees, including others that may not be listed. Use the blank table on the following page to fill in the particular fees that relate to your studies. The minimum amount depends on the student, and the cost of their program. Usually, you will not see a minimum amount due for tuition, as it must be paid either prior to classes starting, or just after. Under rare circumstances, you may be able to set up a payment plan, though you will need to speak with your financial counselor on campus to see if this is possible. Try avoiding this by preparing yourself with obtaining scholarships, grants, and possible sponsorships. When you have these in place, you will not need to have the conversation with your counselor because you cannot pay the fees. You can proudly walk on campus and scream, "My fees are paid because I took the time to search and apply for scholarships!"

What I desire for you to take away from this is to understand that you may not obtain all of the scholarships you have applied for. This is why you must apply for multiple, and learn from the ones you did not get. I am cheering for you, so take the next step and watch things line up for you in the long run.

Blank Table: (Per Semester)

Use a pencil so that you can reuse the following semester.

Invoice Date	Description	Min. Due	Total Owed

Total:

Motivation Corner

The Fantastical Pursuit of Education

I never really knew what to do once high school was over. The only thing I did know was that college was the next step. Fast forward about eight years and four majors, I am now a college graduate with a Bachelor's of Science in Psychology from Clayton State University. During my time finding my calling, I became a wife and mother, and after my first year in college, I relocated. By the next semester, I was pregnant and in school for a vocational certificate so that I could find a job after having my first baby. I was a licensed cosmetologist with a newborn and a new job, and after working for a short while I knew I wanted to further my education. One year later, I received my Associate's in Science degree, but I still had no clue as to what to do with it.

After some soul searching and relocating, my husband, son and I moved to Georgia. I started school with a mission of earning my Psychology degree in the summer of 2010. During the semester I was four months pregnant with my second child, and every year after that I was pregnant as well. I gave birth November 2010, January 2012 and June 2013. I finished classes the week before giving birth to my fourth child, and I walked with the fall 2013 graduating class. As you can see, from beginning to end I was pregnant. I found it very difficult but obtainable. I was a breastfeeding, stay at home mom and full-time student that was beginning my freelance Makeup Artistry business. Although I had a lot on my plate, I enjoyed every class. I love education so I sacrificed my personal time and used it for personal growth. I would not change a thing about that.

The biggest obstacle to overcome is time management. Anything can be done with time management skills. I learned what times of day worked for my learning. I did a lot of night classes and hybrid courses so that I could do work as well as breastfeed, if need be. I also had a wonderful support team that consisted of my mother-in-law and husband. My mother lives out of state, so she donated her time when she could, which by the way, she was also in school earning her first Bachelor's. We graduated the same month within one week of each other. I am glad to have shared that with her.

All I want is for people to be strong in their decisions. If you choose to continue your education, do what it takes to complete that goal. I understand life gets tough and complicated but what would a mountain top be without the rest to hold it up. In order to get to the top there is some climbing involved and it will never be a straight path. To anyone thinking that you may not be able to handle it, do it at your own pace. Do what fits your life for your ultimate goal. My goal of being a Marriage and Family Therapist is in construction at the moment. I am currently a stay at home mom, with a part-time job and freelance Makeup Artist who loves to make YouTube videos. I will soon be adding graduate student to my schedule in the fall of 2015. Remember, you will make time for what you want. If you want it bad enough it will come to life. Anything is possible.

> *Jalea Nicole is a wife, mother of four, make-up artist and visionary. She has received her Bachelors of Science degree in Psychology from Clayton State University. She will be entering Graduate School fall 2015. She currently resides in Atlanta, Georgia where she continues to grow and inspire all.*

Living Costs

When you decide to continue your education it can be a tough decision to make. Let's face it –most people who attend college usually go straight from graduating high school or return to college after many years have gone by. Either way, it can be a financial strain on most individuals wanting to obtain their college degree. The price of living keeps rising, the economy continues to lay off workers only paying the bare minimum with more responsibility, and tuition is sometimes out of our league when you have life responsibilities. Every month you are faced with bills, insurance and rent, and though these are necessities, you get tired of being pulled through the mud. It is not easy when your bank account is scraping by payday after payday, and the one thing that keeps you going is your desire to reach for higher education. The journey is still open, and prayerfully what I share with you in this book will help you to better understand the process of paying for college the way it helped me.

Previously we looked at a brief description of the fees that all students must pay before they can take and complete their classes. Most schools will let you enroll in the class without paying, given that you pay on or before the deadline posted. If you miss this deadline, you will be automatically dropped from your classes or put on a hold status, so please if there are situations prohibiting you from paying your tuition fees, talk to your advisor to avoid being dropped. To go a bit further in the estimated cost, I will now discuss how important it is to understand the price of living.

Most colleges and universities will always factor in the cost of living with the estimated cost of attending that particular school. Pay attention to the difference between living on campus and living off campus. Although the difference may not be much, it can be the difference you need to help pay for other things, such as books. On the next page, I will show you an example of the difference between the two, and how I used it to help pay for other necessities. For those of you who ride public transportation as I have, please factor in that amount where you see transportation.

Sample: (Per Semester)

	On Campus	Off Campus	W/ Parents
Books and Supplies	$1,200	$1,200	$1,200
Meals and Housing	$1,500-$2,000	$500-$1,200	$0 -$600
Personal Expenses	$600	$600	$600
Transportation/Bus	$0	$250- $400	$250- $400
Total:	$3,300-$3,800	$2,550-$3,400	$2,050-$2800

As you can see, the expenses minus tuition can be great living on campus, but it can also be great living off campus. The figures in the table are an estimation of what the university I attended generated based on what I included in my application, FAFSA and so forth, as well as a guesstimate for you to visually see. The school will determine whether you are a dependent or an independent student based on your input, so think cautiously about the information you list. Make sure it is accurate to the best of your knowledge and you are not listing any unnecessary finances that will eliminate funding for you.

For example, someone gave me a monetary gift to help with the cost of some expenses. After speaking to my advisor, I did not list this amount as it would increase the amount of money I am expected to have, and can ultimately lower what I receive. Although there is a section on the FASFA listed as *gifts* you should always speak to a financial counselor at your school to determine if this should be listed. You clearly cannot list every dollar a friend or family member gives you to help, but in certain cases and amounts, you want to make sure that you understand the guidelines set forth when filling out your application. If there is something you do not understand, please DO NOT submit your application before talking to someone. This is why it is important to start you application in advance. It will allow you the opportunity to go over the application as a draft and complete it later. Yes –you can start an application, with a personal pin, and sign back in later to finish where you left off, so do not feel rushed. You want to qualify for as much as you can so that the financial weight of tuition and such can be lifted. As I mentioned earlier, pay attention to the cost of living on/off campus. Here is a personal example of my experience:

During undergrad, I stayed off campus and rented out a room. Although this is much cheaper than staying on campus, I did have to assess what I could pay for. For example, if you look at the table, you will see the difference of about $800-$1000 less for meals and housing between on/off campus. Though this was a rough estimation from the school I attended, I spent more because I paid rent and utilities. Therefore, I had to adjust that amount according to my expenses. Because I lived off campus and paid rent, I spent roughly around $5,000 per semester, which included bills and transportation. What you also have to keep in mind is that everything is on a semester basis, so the living expense and tuition amount should only be calculated per semester, as fees go up, and in some cases so does the rent.

The truth is that those who want to complete their degree also have other financial obligations. If you are wanting to pay for college without the aid of loans, but are limited because of these obligations, then scholarships, grants and sponsorships are your best bet to completing your degree debt free.

Below, I have included a blank table for you to list your fees, as it pertains to your individual circumstance.

Use a pencil so that you can reuse the following semester.

Per Semester

	On Campus	Off Campus	With Parents
Books and Supplies			
Meals and Housing			
Personal Expenses			
Transportation			
Other			

Total:

Financial Aid –Using it wisely

"If you ask people to help fund your education and use the money for other things like clothes and cars –did you really deserve to receive it in the first place?"

I want to use this time to be very open about obtaining financial assistance. I am excited that there are programs that exist for us to get the help needed with school and life choices. I am excited about all of the opportunities that are here to help us propel forward in life. I am excited to say that I have personally experienced some good counselors, professors and financial aid advisors down my path to academic success. This is what keeps me going, and gives me the desire to share information as I have experienced it. It is a proud moment for me. What I am not so excited about is that there are some students who misuse the system to better other areas of their life, instead of applying it to their academics.

Let me explain –I had a friend that was constantly struggling with completing school. I understood that life was hitting her hard, but her mindset was still consumed with the problems she was facing. Semester after semester she would enroll in the local community college and apply for financial aid. I was proud of her for trying to finish school, so that was not the problem. The problem was noticed during a conversation we were having about paying for college. My friend would describe to me that it was financially hard to pay for school and that she could not do it without assistance. I agreed because neither could I afford school without help. One day we were talking and she began to tell me about how she received her financial aid check in the mail. The first thought that came to my mind was, "that's great". My friend went on to say that instead of getting books she went and bought herself a whole new wardrobe, and purchased a car off the street. My heart dropped because after our previous discussion of how hard it is to pay for college, I expected her to buy all of her school necessities because this is what the money was for.

This takes me back to changing your mindset. You have to want it in your mind first before you actually see it manifest. My friend's mind was on taking the money and doing as she desired, instead of doing what was needed. Not long after she was put on financial aid restriction. Although she got away with it semester after semester, her education was being cheated because she did not have the tools needed to perform in the classroom, which presented low grades and a red alert to the financial aid office. Yes, they will suspend your assistance if your grades are not up to par.

There are so many students applying for college with a desire to actually study and graduate, some desiring to transfer. You can do as you wish with the money you receive, but just keep in mind that it is needed for those seeking to use it for its sole purpose. If you believe that you are not going to actually use the money for school necessities, consider not accepting the offer so that the money can be there for someone who actually needs it.

As we move on, I want to recap on things we have discussed. Here are other forms of financial assistance you do not have to pay back:

1. Financial Aid: Complete application BEFORE deadline every year (also check website to see any changes in dates).
    a. www.studentaid.ed.gov/FAFSA
    b. This is FREE to apply for, so make sure you take advantage.
2. Cal Grant A and B
3. State University Grant
4. Federal Work Study (see your campus office)
5. Book Grants
6. EOPS Programs (most provide stipends or extra cash)
7. Pell Grant

Helpful Tip:

Budget cuts: Be leery of return grants. Colleges will deduct this amount from your financial award without you knowing.
I learned the hard way.

Personal Motivation

"Why would anybody put chains on power? Well, that's what happens when you doubt your ability to succeed."

Never stop believing even when it seems like all odds are against you! During my undergrad years, I would write personal notes to myself. I spent many days frustrated because I was not making much money working a job ($7.50 an hour) and only getting between 3-10 hours a week, if that. For some reason, I believed that my supervisor at that time had a personal vendetta against me to where she would only give me three hours in a week knowing I was a struggling student. I would get so frustrated because I had just moved to a new area, was staying with someone but still paying rent, had bills piling up, had just lost my storage with everything I owned in the world in it, and felt like things were just going downhill.

On top of that, I struggled with paying for school, but never gave up on graduating. I was determined that even if it took me ten years to finish community college, I was going to do it. I envisioned myself walking the stage with my cap and gown on, and eventually fought my way through. One thing that helped to motivate me was to write personal notes to myself. You may be thinking to yourself, *is this necessary?* Although for some it may not be, others can benefit from doing this. When you are going through certain situations in life, and it feels like you can't make it, writing letters to yourself is a way to keep you going. I know for a fact that if I had not written constant letters during some of the hardest struggles and encounters I faced, I would not have made it through. You have to understand that when you can write everything you need to do on paper, it becomes easier to accomplish. By writing positive affirmations, you are creating a way of escape on paper that you will be able to tangibly walk through.

You may remember my story in the beginning of this book, but here is one of my personal notes below that I wrote during some challenging times:

Dear Toi,

The easiest thing for you to do is give up. Quitting is never hard when it comes to your dreams because you get tired, and in return you give up.

Education has always been something you wanted to accomplish, but it seems like it is impossible to make it to the finish line. You are barely an adult, twenty years old, and you have so many dreams for yourself that it is beginning to feel heavy. Please, for the sake of our future, keep going. You are working this job right now because you need to, and although you are overworked and underpaid, you will learn valuable lessons in the end. I know that it is tough not having any help, or people helping you to succeed. You may not understand now, but you will make it through this. I cannot say when, but you will complete your degree and go places that you only dreamed of. I believe that there will be people who will enter into your life to push you forward. It may hurt at times, but it will strengthen you. Do me a favor will you? Do not stop at community college, reach for the university. I know that it appears far from your reach, but take it one step at a time. Get back up when you have fallen, and no matter what, do not give up on your dreams. I believe that we can do this.

The year I received my first degree in May 2011 (Associate Degree of Liberal Arts and Humanities).

Motivation Corner

When Faith Gives You Victory!

My name is Shantelle Ortiz. I am twenty-one years old, and currently a graduate student-athlete at Saint Mary's College in Moraga, California. I recently graduated from the University Of San Francisco (class of 2015). My journey was not easy but with the grace of GOD, I MADE IT! Just a little background of where I come from. I was born is San Francisco, California but I was raised and spent the majority of my elementary school years in Los Angeles. I moved back to Northern California my fifth grade year. My journey really began in high school, where I attended North Hills Baptist Christian High school for my freshman and sophomore year and for my junior and senior year I attended Calvary Missionary Baptist High school. I was a student athlete at both high schools playing basketball and soccer. I knew I wanted to play soccer in college because I have been playing soccer for 18 years. I started my college journey at Diablo Valley College in Pleasant Hill, California where I was also a student-athlete. I majored in criminal justice because I plan to join the California Highway Patrol. I had my college years planned out, but things did not go the way I expected and wanted them to go, being that my plan was to transfer after two years.

    As I mentioned before, I played soccer at Diablo Valley College and I was determined to continue on in collegian sports. Everything had seemed to go smoothly with my grades and soccer until the end of my first year. My soccer team made playoffs and it was the semi-final game. It was a very intense game and toward the end of the first half I got a knee injury and I did not think it was as bad as it was. I tried to finish the game but the pain got worse. After getting the test done, I found out I tore my MCL and if I had kept on playing I would have torn my ACL. After Two surgeries I was out for 6 weeks and things began to get rough for me for sports and for school. My GPA dropped from a 3.75 to a 3.45. I was put on my team's Disabled List for the following season, which meant I would not be able to play the next season at all. I felt like it was the end for me and all hope was gone. I knew no colleges would recruit me for soccer because of my grades and I was out for my sophomore and final Junior College season. I started to stress about the financial portion of school, and how everything was going to work out. I ended up doing two and a half years at DVC.

One Sunday at church my Bishop taught on faith and that day my spirit began to rise and I knew that if I put my faith in Christ any and all things are possible. I prayed and told the LORD to let HIS will be done and if HE wanted this for me HE will do it. The following Tuesday, I went outside to get the mail and it was a pretty heavy stack. After I looked through the mail and nothing was for me, I let my spirit get down again. The mailman came back to my house with another stack and said "I am sorry ma'am I forgot to give you the rest of your mail" and I didn't think any of it was for me. I looked through the pile and I had a total of 10 schools who had already recruited me for soccer from my freshman year. Those schools included University of San Francisco, Saint John's in New York, University of Miami, Florida, University of Texas, University of California at Los Angeles, and New Mexico State. I committed to the University of San Francisco. I caught up with my school work and I finished my career at DVC with a 3.75.

I went on to the University of San Francisco for my next two years. I told myself that I will keep my grades up regardless of my job, soccer, and any other extra-curricular activities. I did so as I promised myself and my parents. I worked at *InShape* gym for my two years at USF. It was not easy at all because I worked from 3:50 a.m. – 9 a.m. in the morning, went to school, had soccer practice or a game and on non-game days I would work a split shift (3:50 a.m. -9 a.m. then 5 p.m.-9 p.m.). It got rough for a little while after only averaging 2 ½ to 3 hours of sleep but I was determined to get my school work done while maintaining a job and soccer. I did finish the school year on a good note. I graduated with a 3.5 as a student-athlete and received my bachelors in criminal justice and now I will be attending Saint Mary's college in the fall to get my masters in accounting. I will play my last year of soccer, while working for the Golden State Warriors in the financial department and Front desk at a 4 Star Hotel. I would not have been able to do any of this without my LORD and Savior JESUS CHRIST, my Parents, Church Family, and other Family and friends. If I can do it anyone can do it! You have to put your faith and trust that the LORD will come through for you.

Shantelle Ortiz is a graduate from the University of San Francisco with a Bachelor's of Arts degree in Criminal Justice. She is currently pursuing her Master's degree in Accounting from Saint Mary's College. She will be starting her program with the California Highway Patrol in December 2015.

THE PROCESS

"I began to use my love for writing as the key to crafting a wonderful essay, coupled with the strength of my background as a disadvantaged minority".

Going through a process in life can be draining. No matter what you do, there are going to be certain steps you need to take in order to move forward. The process in applying for scholarships comes with many stages, some we often overlook or try to skip over. This is why it is important that you start as early as possible so that you can avoid the stress, or at least some of it.

I have to admit that I was all over the place in the beginning stages in applying for scholarships. I did not know what I was doing and did not have help, so initially I kept coming to a brick wall. It took me a few years to get back on track, and when I did there was no stopping me. I began to take my time with researching out the proper scholarships that would give me a chance to show what I was about. I challenged myself to maintain a personal level of self-development and pushed myself to ask as many questions necessary for my success. I went through an immediate growth spurt, so to say. I began to use my love for writing as the key to crafting a wonderful essay, coupled with the strength of my background as a disadvantaged minority. You have to use what you already have, and develop who you are when you feel odds are against you. The steps in writing an essay starts with simple questions and learning to rewrite until it works.

Because you are reading this book, you or someone you know have decided to apply for scholarships and now you're ready to write the best essay you have ever written. This process can be time consuming, but with the right questions and information, you can begin to dig deep to pull out that hidden essay resting inside of you. For me personally, writing is something that I study, so I enjoyed the process. Here are a few questions I asked myself before I started writing:

1. What are my academic goals?
2. What are my personal goals?
3. Where do I see myself in the near future?
4. How do I want to give back to my community?
5. What have I learned from past experiences?
6. What challenges have I had in the past? How did I overcome them?
7. What is my background? Were both of my parents in the home? How did this effect my studies and personal life?
8. What degree am I pursuing?
9. What is my plan of action?
10. What schools am I searching to attend?

Below, list a few of your goals you may want to discuss in your essay. This can help you develop a strong personal statement to the scholarship board. I have done the first one for you as an example:

Personal Goals Table

EX: *To maintain a 3.5 GPA or higher as a commitment to pursue my degree in psychology.*

HOW TO WRITE AN ESSAY

*"Sometimes it is not easy to write about
your life and goals, but how can others see your vision
of success, if you don't."*

When writing an essay you have to be very careful not to lose focus on what is being asked of you. I am no scholarly professional, but it is very important to pay attention to the questions that are asked by the scholarship panel because it will determine if your essay meets the relevant criteria. What you do not want to do is write out of eagerness. Instead, take your time developing what you want to say, how you want to say it, and in what order it needs to be delivered. Most people find themselves stuck on beginning their essay because they do not know how to start it. I would suggest that you first pay closer attention to the questions that the interview panel lists, and go from there by answering each question accordingly. Once you have completed this task, you can begin to create your intro. The intro of your essay is basically the only opportunity you have to grab your reader's attention. In the intro it is important to be creative, while making sure that you openly give your reader a reason to continue with your essay. Let's take a look at some points to discuss in the intro below:

Beginning

Intro/key points you want to discuss.

- ✓ Who are you? (Be brief, but specific).
- ✓ State the basis of your essay, relevant and key points.
- ✓ Introduce the subject at hand (wanting to pursue higher education and the need you have).

An example of this would be:

My willingness and desire to go after my dreams are relevant to my need. I am an independent student seeking to seize every opportunity which comes my way, but my financial need is much greater.

Usually, the intro forces your reader to read more. It is okay to use proper notated quotes from other authors, but try to limit your quote usage. There is a correct way to do this, which you will have an opportunity to see in Essay Example #1. Always remember that the selection panel is interested in getting to know you, not the quoted author.

Body

Discuss those key points noted above here.

- ✓ Answer essay questions given by scholarship or university panel.
- ✓ Be authentic in your response, not forgetting to be yourself.
- ✓ Limit yourself from being a charity case. Remember that you are a hard worker who is seeking an opportunity, not a hand-out.
- ✓ Incorporate your intro into the body of your essay.
- ✓ Discuss your challenges, but stress how you have overcome.

An example of this would be:

One of the most difficult challenges I have had to face in life was being homeless. This taught me the value of life and hard work, and while these challenges could have broken me, they did not. Instead, I constantly strive to be an advocate for homelessness, and to provide assistance and leadership to the community at large.

Notice the paragraph above. It clearly discusses someone experiencing a difficult challenge. One thing I want you to notice is that the reader does not have time to feel sorry for the individual because it is crafted in a way that determines a better outcome.

Conclusion

Make the reader believe in you.

- ✓ Your dreams matter –STATE THEM.
- ✓ Discuss how you desire to use your degree.
- ✓ Show how getting into the school of your choice and being selected for a scholarship would benefit you.
- ✓ Show your plan of action (i.e. campus tours, meeting with counselors.
- ✓ ALWAYS thank the reader in closing.

An example of this would be:

Currently, I am pursuing volunteer/intern positions in my field of study so that I can gain valuable experience. I have scheduled a few campus tours, and have met with my counselor to determine the final steps during this transition. Upon graduation, I desire to fully engage myself in the workforce, while being a valuable asset to the community.

The closing paragraph(s) should always sum up your essay. Never overextend what you have already said to the point where it feels heavy. For example, you do not have to continue stating that you were homeless, or that you were raised by a single parent, unless it is absolutely necessary. I can never stress this enough –ALWAYS thank the reader for the opportunity.

An example of this would be:

I thank you in advance for the opportunity you have given myself and like-minded students, and for providing a source of assistance for higher education.

Helpful Tip:

When writing your essay be transparent as possible, but DO NOT make yourself look like a charity case. From my experience, those who are on the committee reading your essay want to see your growth, and how you did not allow yourself to be limited by circumstance. Be the change, instead of being engulfed by it!

Below, I have included sample scholarship essays, which I call one of them *the pillar that got me through*. I say this because the first essay alone have helped me obtain many scholarships, and have left professors stopping me in the hall asking me questions like, "who taught you how to write like that?" Your essay should be powerful enough that teachers will enjoy reading your work. When you read the sample essays, please understand that plagiarism is a serious matter, so use it as a guide to help you with your own story. Also, for publication reasons I have taken out the names of the university, but remember to list the name of the school you are going to in your essay. Now that you know the basics in writing an essay, let's take a look at some sample essays on the following page.

Sample Essay #1

Ralph Waldo Emerson once said, "People fail to see that their perception of the world is also a confession of character." I often wonder what it means to have character, and what it is I am confessing. Who I have become is a mere product of the environment I have created. The environment did not create me. I say this because my backyard not only bore the streets of Hollywood and Beverly Hills, the infamous fairytale of fame and wealth. The four walls of my backyard also included violence, homelessness, religion and the eager struggle to survive the mean streets of South Central, or for a better choice of words, Los Angeles –the place which is called *The city of Angels*.

Through it all I fought for my life; the mental me, the spiritual me, the physical and verbal me. Every single part of my life was dying and with great anticipation: ready to die. I can only be truthful in saying this: I have played a major part in this journey because I did not understand that everything attached to my life was the foundation which gave me reason to believe that a healthy destiny was so far out of reach it was impossible to obtain. This contributed to my verbal communication, or the lack thereof, and instead of taking challenge by the bullhorns and changing my outcome, I became challenged.

I start this essay off with the above passage because there are many stories to be told in life, and in all respect I have an obligation to speak out those challenges so that everyone can see a difference. I was raised by a single mother, working two jobs: a janitor, cleaning the left behind dirt of someone else's footprints by day, and a nurse tending to the needs of a helpless soul by night. My mother broke her back serving the needs of others, which left my family depending on non-tradition, painful communication, and running away from the issue to only create new ones. There was no father around, but when my three sisters and I did see him, he was unfamiliar, abusive and not worthy of our respect. Struggle has always been a big part of my life, regardless of my dreams, but it did not keep me there.

Violence within the family taught me something no one else could. It taught me the opposite of my reality. I knew that I wanted better for myself and I did not want to become another statistic of my environment taking advantage of laziness. I had to create my environment through my imagination to be a support system for change. I took the present reality, gave it life through a pencil and made sure that the moments I experienced growing up were only stepping stones to life's stairway. My imagination pushed me to the edge of the cliff, like an escape clause, when homelessness came knocking at my door in elementary school. I understood then that opportunity was on its way. I needed to know that prostitution on the street corners was not my reality. I needed to understand that sleeping on a park slide when homelessness took a picture of me and tried to keep my soul within its image was not the photograph I was supposed to be in. I needed to be brave enough to know that I was weak in thinking that opportunity was searching to personally shake hands and meet me. I find myself, more so now, in being a liberal for my freedom. I challenge change to build a mountain in front of me and watch as I climb it. In some ways you become the product of your environment and can end up either way in life –not caring to grow, or striving to get out, which is true. I became the product of my wanting to understand the reality of who I was and be understood by it as well.

One of the most defining times in my life was only a few short years ago. In June of 2007 I went through a situation that left me homeless sleeping on a park slide in my hometown of Los Angeles, California. I would wait until it got dark enough and the parents took their kids' home for dinner that I would make my move up the blue padded stairs on the yellow open slide. I had my big pink polka-dot backpack with a few clothes in it to cushion my head as a pillow, and the sweater on my arms to embrace me as covers. I was twenty-four years old when this happened and even now I look back at the situation and I find myself understanding that if I had not gone through that experience I would not have learned to fight when challenge came up against me.

After those chilly nights of making a bed out of a child's playground, I began to envision myself as a whole person –healthy, happy and thankful, and in that moment my life changed forever. I became determined and utterly strengthened to change the lives of those who will come after me. It was then that I began to take my life seriously. For once, I decided to grow and not be hindered by homelessness or the physical abuse of molestation I encountered as a child. Instead, I made it my personal testimony and began to step out of my comfort zone to reach out to other young teen girls who are burdened with their childhood. I have gained confidence in my integrity because I am not afraid of hearing the word *No*; knowing that I have the ability to create my *own Yes*.

Regardless of my finances, I have learned to pinch pennies for my dream. In 2007, that same year, I gathered every dime I had to self-publish my first book of poetry *Mirror to my Soul*. My second book *The Hush Language* came shortly after because I was determined for my dream even while making a minimum wage income. The lessons I have learned out of pain is that I have grown in humility and faith. My faith is in God, not man; my humility is in overcoming, not the obstacle, and my perseverance lies in my ability to continue. Challenge has taught me the necessity of serving others. This is why I have volunteered my time at New Birth Church in Pittsburg, California through the Literacy department to help strengthen the verbal education in our communities. Through this program I am able to open the voices of not only youth, but those of all ages. It is funny, or rather amazing because when I was younger I did not have perfect communication skills, and today I am teaching others how to present themselves through the form of writing.

I tell myself all the time: I have everything inside of me to complete my journey. I represent the idea. I represent the possibility and in those times I get pushed to the edge, I do not wait for the push –I jump and begin to soar in the possibility.

I fought for my life to secure the mental me, to embrace the spiritual me, to strengthen the physical me, to appreciate the verbal me –and to this day I am still fighting because I am a whole and unique individual who chooses to keep going. My desire and life's purpose is to not only continue my education through the undergraduate program while studying Creative Writing, but to also take a higher step in continuing on to Graduate School to further enhance my career goals. I do believe in serving the needs of people through whatever outlet you are capable of doing so, and sharing with them the knowledge of overcoming so that they can take the necessary steps needed to accomplish their goals and dreams. You cannot succeed in higher education without the proper support, finances and motivation; this is why I would be honored to receive this scholarship and your support to continue bettering my life through education, while allowing myself to be used towards the benefit of others. I realize now what it is that I am confessing; it is only that obstacle does not have to be the thing that has destroyed me, but that which has wakened me.

I thank you in advance for seeing the need of students by providng financial support, and for allowing me to finish what I started.

Sample Essay #2

I believe that life, itself, is here to present opportunity, watching to see what we make of it. If I could describe myself in one word, I would say: overcomer. I believe that many people know how to fight when life is hard, but there are plenty of people who get tired of fighting and give up. This is what I know for sure –I am a fighter, and I do not give life permission to make me quit.

During my academic journey, I graduated from the community college with my Associate's degree in Liberal Arts and Humanities. During this time, I received a Certitificate of Achievement in the Professional Career Program at the community college, and was asked by the scholarship office to be their speaker of the hour for the awards ceremony. Upon transferring to University, I received several other scholarships to help with the cost. It was then that I understood the signifance of education and the importance of struggle being an ingredient for strength. I am part of the Study Abroad office, where I have volunteered this summer by providing information based on my study abroad experinces this past year. The information I sumbmitted is now part of the study abroad office archive, and will be utilized as information for students planning to apply to study in another country.

For my final year of studies at the University, I decided to go out and do something I never had the chance to do. I decided to journey across the waters to the United Kingdom and enter into another country to finish my senior year of Undergrad. With this, I have received the Gilman Scholarship to help pay the cost of traveling abroad, and it has allowed me to study and see places that I could only dream of.

In 2009, I started working in the community with an outreach program in Pittsburg, CA with the Literacy department to help promote and maintain pertinent curriculums and programs. These programs were geared towards youth and adult minorities who need the extra support in developing a solid background in learning to read, which were also reinforced by individual tutoring and mentorship. The passion beyond these programs helped me to understand that the community at large has a demand for help. I wish to strengthen my background experiences in the nonprofit and public sectors by positioning myself in the community through various outlets. I desire to be part of the process in making informed decisions for minorities who feel that their voices go unheard. Because of this, I have a strong desire to bridge myself into the academic systems while helping to promote positive change.

My personal goals are to find internships in non-profit sectors where I can gain the experience and knowledge of the needs of the community, while also bettering my social skills needed to succeed in Graduate Studies. In this, I desire to work closely with individuals and organizations already working in Public Administration, so that it will better my chances of understanding the principles of organizational demands in the work force. I do not agree with any statistic that speaks of youth not being able to succeed because of their challenging backgrounds and circumstances. I have learned to use my drive and desire to go beyond those statistics.

Instead, I have decided to become a solution to the on-going crisis by lending my personal experiences as a platform to reach those in underprivileged communities to go higher in their education. If someone like me can start at the bottom where homelessness and abuse were prevalent in my upbringing and turn things around, surely there are opportunities for others to do the same. It does take persistence and determination to continue reaching for your dreams when you have been told no so many times, but the reward is worth the fight. In the near future as I come to completion with Graduate School, I desire to give back to my community through scholarships and academic mentoring to help those who are struggling with applying for scholarships. Along with my desire to mentor youth and to help provide access in the educational system to those who are at a disadvantage, I also have an interest to work in urban planning where I can continue to provide solutions to the crisis and help to develop strategic plans that will build better communities for the future.

Obtaining this degree will provide me with the opportunity to find my place in the world, while building character that will allow me to pursue change over opposition. I believe that I need the teachings of your program to help me achieve these goals. By being part of the (MPA) Program, I will be able to gain the experience needed, while learning from those who can guide me in the right direction. I also believe that education is a powerful tool, and can help me to get through doors that are otherwise hard to enter.

Since the completion of my Bachelor's degree and my study abroad experiences in the United Kingdom, I have seen first-hand how other countries view the American population. Having the opportunity to live and learn from other countries allowed me to develop a built-in motivation to succeed in whatever I set my mind to. This is why I believe that entering the Public Administration program is the right time. This opportunity will allow me to keep the momentum going, while being an encouragement for others to do the same. As President Barack Obama declared, I desire to 'reignite the engine of America's growth' and I personally challenge change to build a mountain in front of me and watch as I climb it in the process.

I thank you in advance for giving me the opportunity to be the change and difference I want to see in the community, and for helping me to continue flourishing in the next level of my education.

Sample Essay #3

Life has never been easy for me, and because of personal experiences I encourntered growing up, I planted my feet in the educational system, first starting with community college. It was a challenge in the beginning because it was hard to focus on school when I had to work a full-time job to support myself, but I stuck with it. On May 2011, I graduated from Los Medanos community college with my Associate's degree in Liberal Arts and Humanities. I also received a Certitificate of Achievement in the Professional Career Program at the community college, and was asked by the scholarship office to be their speaker of the hour for the awards ceremony. Upon transferring to the University, I received numerous scholarships that would carry me. It was then that I understood the signifance of education and the importance of struggle being an indgredient to gain strength. Here at the University I am part of the Study Abroad office, where I will be volunteering this coming fall, as well as the International Education Exchange Council (IEEC) and the Associated Students Inc. (ASI). I have contributed to volunteering in the community in my major field, while teaching a Poetry and Creative Writing course at my church in Pittsburg, California over a three year period. The classes were an opportuntiy to help promote literacy by putting on poetry events in the community where I hosted the events as well, and taught a range of students from various ages how to read.

    For my final year of studies at the University, I decided to go out and do something I never had the chance to do. I decided to journey across the waters to the United Kingdom and enter into another country to finish my senior year of Undergrad. I am currently here in England, and at this very moment something is rising up inside of my veins pushing me to go further. With this, I received an additional scholarship to help pay the cost of traveling abroad, and it has allowed me to study and see places that I could only dream of. This coming May, I will be a participant in the commencement ceremony to receive my Bachelor's degree.

My personal goals are to find internships in the local school systems where I can gain the experience and knowledge of teaching Creative Writing, while also bettering my social skills needed to succeed in Graduate Studies this coming fall. In this, I desire to work closely with grade school youth because my mission is to promote literacy at an early age, so that children can grow to become great writers, leaders, visionaries and philosophers. I do not agree with any statistic that speaks of youth not being able to succeed because of their challenging backgrounds and circumstances. Instead, I have decided to become a solution to the on-going statistic by lending my personal experiences as a platform to reach those in underprivileged communities to go higher in their education. If someone like me can start at the bottom where homelessness and abuse were prevalent in my upbringing and turn things around, surely there are opportunities for others to do the same. It does take persistence and determination to continue reaching for your dreams when you have been told no so many times, but the reward is worth the fight.

In the near future, I desire to give back to my community through scholarships and academic mentoring to help those who are struggling with applying for scholarships because they are unaware of how to start. I have a desire to mentor youth and to help provide access in the educational system that will focus on helping students financially and academically to achieve their goals.

By receiving this award, I will be one step closer to being a better example for those who are just starting out in their academics, as well as those returning. This award will allow me to not only continue my studies in Graduate School, but it is an encouragement for me to continue down this academic path where I am becoming a better person each day. I can no longer say that the problems I had as a youth hindered me from growing because I have grown. Those situations have pushed me to mature and to challenge myself when I did not think that I would make it. I am living proof that it can be done if you are consistent in wanting to be better than your past, and greater than your circumstance. I thank you in advance for giving me the opportunity to share my story, and to continue flourishing in the next level of my life.

Sample Essay #4

The morals and values I want to develop must outlive me, and resonate in the minds of our next generation. I was going back and forth with having this perception that I had to be what everyone else wanted me to be; though I decided against this. As a matter of fact, I decided against a lot of things which led me on this journey in trying to understand in full what I wanted. The main lesson that I have learned over the past couple of years is that challenge is the connection to being developed and stretched in ways that forces you to grow. Therefore, I forced myself in being challenged in writing what I have never written, and to explore what I have never explored.

My personal goals are to find internships in the local school systems where I can gain the experience and knowledge of teaching what I have learned, while also bettering my social skills needed to succeed in continuing my education. In this, I desire to work closely with grade school youth because my mission is to promote literacy at an early age, so that children can grow to become great writers, leaders, visionaries and philosophers.

In the beginning, I challenged everything in my upbringing because I did not quite understand my connection to it all. What am I here for? How do I determine where I fit in? I am the type of person that stands on the edge of the cliff, not waiting for someone to push me over it, but I stand there waiting for the right time to jump into my own possibility. I feel that if you never take a chance in your life, and go for those things that may seem unreachable, you will never be able to fully understand who you are. This is why I applied for this scholarship the first time. I was given an opportunity to reach for something I could only envision in my mind, but I still pushed myself not knowing that I would be selected as a recipient of the award.

I have definitely continued on this path where I create my own possibility and outcome in the situation, while pushing myself in not becoming a prisoner to my dreams. Although I have become used to doing it alone, I do have certain people around that help me celebrate the beginning and end of the things I reach for. I have learned to deliberately take steps towards what I want to accomplish in life, and no matter what may happen the most important thing is that I took a step.

I know first-hand what the financial support from an organization can do. If I had not received the funds to further my education in the previous year, I would not have had the extra support to spread my wings wider than my dreams. I understand that when it comes to most scholarships there are many qualified students competing, so I am standing before you through this essay as someone who not only deserves your support, but appreciates it as well. I choose to continue pushing myself to go beyond in my education despite the many obstacles that I face. I am not the type of person that receives a scholarship and turn away from the people that privileged me with the necessary funds to survive. Instead, I have really begun to look at ways to eventually start my own scholarship support system. In the near future, I desire to give back to my community through scholarships and academic mentoring to help those who are struggling with applying for scholarships because they are unaware of how to start.

There is no better way to end this by saying: I am almost done – can see the finish line right in front of me, and I am ready to take the next step into greater things.

In some cases, organizations giving the scholarship will ask you to submit a publication summary with your essay. This is not a sign that you have been chosen, but it is helpful just in case you are the recipient. The publication summary will be listed in promotional material by the scholarship organization such as, pamplets, books etc. They will have you sign a waiver of release upon notification of your award. Below, I have listed my version of the publication summary to help you along the way. Usually, it is a short description of who you are, what school you are attending, and your goals going forward.

Sample:

Publication Summary

Although I am a current Senior at San Francisco State University studying in my field of English: Creative Writing; I have taken a step further academically where I am presently an International student at the University of East Anglia in Norwich, England. Being in a new country have taught me the definition of perseverance and determination to push through obstacle. I am preparing to graduate this spring and look forward to Graduate School the following year.

Helpful Tip:

When writing your publication summary, stay within the short word limit they give you. If you are over a few words try to eliminate a word that is not really necessary, but just takes up space.

Sample Sponsorship Letter

Cover Letter

Honored Sponsor:

I am pleased to submit this request for your review. I look forward to your partnership in my effort to strive for higher education at the University this fall. My main purpose and goal is to secure my financial future and above all to place a demand on my destiny.

I continue to express a certain level of confidence which creates an example of perseverance and drive to those who have seen my faithfulness. I have the passion, the drive, and the fight to become a success in my field of study: Literature/Creative Writing, and look forward to sharing my story with you in the coming weeks. I have enclosed a letter and Financial Statement for your consideration in hopes that you will take the time to see my need and follow through.

I thank you in advance for taking the time and for giving me this opportunity of higher education.

Actual Sample Letter

Honored Sponsor:

This coming fall, I will be stepping out on faith in the desire to complete my Bachelors of Arts degree at the University. Right now, I am completing the necessary transfer units and taking advantage of all necessary programs that can assist in the transfer process. With an acceptance letter in hand to the University and the strong will and determination to continue being focused, it has become a challenging pursuit to secure the tuition needed to accomplish these goals.

Over the past few years my main desire was to secure my identity and establish sound goals intended to help me grow in the midst of economic turmoil and lack of support. Though there are challenges of community college fees raising per unit and plans to increase later this year, the lack of job positions and the secure foundation of overcoming, I am not giving up on the one thing that pushes me closer to my dreams: Education. My degree of choice and divine instruction is Literature/Creative Writing, which again I have been accepted into the writing program at a time when numerous applicants were denied. My ultimate goal is to learn under the instruction of the professional staff and their expertise of language and literary arts.

Because there are limited resources available, aside from meeting the criteria of Financial Aid, Cal Grants and Scholarships, which I have already applied for, I have begun to take matters into my own hands with the request of asking for help. Please, I need your help. Attached you will find a Financial Statement of Tuition needed and contact information on where you can send your donation. If you would like to join in supporting the higher education strive of my success, please respond via phone, email or written statement to the contact listed with this letter.

If granted this opportunity to be sponsored by you, my contribution to society will be that much greater. I will be given an even greater opportunity to open myself more to be a vessel to those who may need assistance in the future. Thank you for considering this request for your financial support, and for helping me to not only continue my education but to strengthen my gifts and talents for the betterment of my future. If you have any questions about this request or need more information, please do not hesitate to contact me.

Please be aware that fees are continuously increasing and are subject to change overtime; therefore any assistance you are capable of donating is well accepted and appreciated. Thank you in advance for your time and investment into my future.

Grateful,

(Include name here)

Helpful Tip:

You can attach Financial Statement of Tuition Need on the next page, if you desire. This is your opportunity to show the fees needed.

Please Note:

Include your contact information below the letter, so all sponsors will know where to send donations.

Attached to the letter you can include a copy of the financial breakdown of what it will cost you to attend school per semester. This will give those you are sending the letter to a good list of financial obligations, and how they can help. To see a sample of the financial breakdown I have included in this book, please refer to previous chapter (page 28) for a list of student fees.

You can also send an additional cost form attached to your sponsorship request letter. This is just another way to state what finances are needed. Please see a sample sheet below:

Additional Costs:	**List amount here**
Increase in tuition (if any)	
Additional books needed	
Extra fees, such as daycare for parents	

Sample Scholarship Sheet

Discouraged about Mediocre grades?
It is still possible to get scholarships.

Scholarship	Amount	Deadline	Contact info

Note: The above table has been edited and decreased in size for publishing purposes. You can obtain a blank scholarship form from your scholarship office to keep track of what you have applied for, and the result of your submissions.

Motivation Corner

NEVER QUIT. NEVER QUIT. NEVER QUIT.

Trust in the Lord with all your heart, lean not to your own understanding and in all your ways acknowledge Him and he will direct your path – Proverbs 3:5-6

This scripture kept me. I was 15 years old when I had my first son and in the 10th grade. Every single statistic was against me completing high school let alone attending college. But God! I was a survivor and nothing could stop me – or so I thought. I managed to finish high school and start college with a full ride scholarship in hand. I quit during the first year – I just had my second child and school was just too much. I needed to work. I had come from an extremely abusive childhood. I was emotionally and physically abused, molested and raped. I lived a life filled with prostitution, rejection, low self-esteem, hopelessness and poverty. I believed a lie that no one cared about me and that I would never return to school and get a degree. Growing up in a life filled with horrible choices after another and a lifestyle rife with drugs, addictions, hopelessness and poverty took its toll.

It took me over 10 years to return to school. But if I could do it – then so can you. I finished my Bachelor's degree through an accelerated program at University of Phoenix and will be continuing my education this fall. In the next five years I plan to complete my Doctorate degree in Education.

After I finished my Bachelor's degree I realized that I needed to get my children ready. I co-founded a program to specifically help parents learn what it takes to get their students to and through college. Through this program, I have had the privilege of helping hundreds of young people get to college.

MY ADVICE TO YOU

1. Believe in yourself.
2. Don't let money be your excuse.
   a. Research and apply to every scholarship you can.
   b. Visit your career center at your high school.
   c. Network with people and ASK for their help.
   d. Talk to people who are where you want to be and ask for their help.
3. Volunteer for research projects.
4. Stay away from negative people.
5. Ask for help – colleges are filled with people just waiting to help you.

Dear Heart – Please know that I believe in you with all my heart. You can do this and there is nothing and no one that can stop you. I believe in you!

> *Darice A. Ingram dual majored in Management and Administration from the University of Phoenix. Darice is an Education Consultant, and co-founder of Parents Connected. She currently lives in the Bay Area and has plans of completing her Doctorate degree in Education.*

Scholarship Fact Sheet

"Given the fact that I was brought up as low-income, society says I'm supposed to be a statistic, but I challenge that because I am not defined by the struggle."

Having a scholarship fact sheet will allow you to easily navigate through the process. If you can clearly see on paper what needs to be done, then you will have a better opportunity at not becoming overwhelmed with the task. When applying for schools and scholarships, it can be stressful. The most important thing is to keep track of everything you do. In the fact sheet below, I have listed some of the main requirements needed during this process, some of which must be done before you can move on to the next level. Ask yourself these questions:

- Have you completed the FAFSA application by the deadline?
- Have you completed the necessary application forms?
- Have you written your personal statement/essay in a timely manner?

If not, then you know what you need to do. If you have, then just check it off the list and move on to the next. Do what works for you, but this technique helps to simplify the process.

Also, please understand that this is one of my personal techniques that I have used during undergrad. It was helpful to me, and I know will be helpful to you.

Item	Revise/Edit	Completed	Date
FAFSA	☐	☐	
Application Form	☐	☐	
GPA Verified (seniors ONLY)	☐	☐	
Personal Statement	☐	☐	
Recommendation Letters (3 min.)	☐	☐	
Academic Resume (Most Require)	☐	☐	

Helpful Tip:

Make sure to always edit and revise your work before you submit. The last thing you need is to have your application rejected because you have not checked your grammar.

The Interview Process

*"When one door closes and you can't see the window
–pick the lock."*

Having an interview is one of the most important steps to getting into the university and/or obtaining a scholarship. It is vital that you take this time to prepare yourself by doing mock interviews. If you are uncomfortable in interviews, try getting together with someone you know, or a counselor to give you a mock interview by asking you questions pertaining to your application. It may seem uncomfortable at first, but it will help to prepare you for the real thing. There are also opportunities on campus that will allow you to attend workshops to help strengthen your verbal communication skills. Take advantage of it! The community college and university I attended both had workshops that helped to prepare students for the interview process. Here are some techniques I learned that will make you more comfortable, and give you a better chance at receiving scholarships. Please note, the below information is what I learned personally, and is just a mere fraction of other techniques you may come in contact with to assist you.

Interviewing Techniques

- ✓ Interview panel
    - o Get to know the scholarship panel by doing some research. Most scholarships will list those who will serve on the panel.
    - o Ask questions. There is nothing worse than a silent mouse.
    - o Be yourself. They know that you may be nervous, but there is no reason to show it.
    - o Bring any necessary documents that is requested, i.e. acceptance letter of university attending.

- ✓ Dress code

    - o Be professional.
    - o Do not wear skirts that are inappropriate, or shorts to the interview.
    - o Civic attire (black and white) always work.
    - o Do not put on perfume or cologne. They want to meet you, not smell you from a distance.
    - o Leave jeans for another day.

- ✓ Arrive Early

    - o Show up a ½ hour early or more if possible.
    - o Find the location of your interview.
    - o Locate the restrooms, and use them upon arrival.
    - o Greet the staff in the hall.
    - o Some group interviews may provide snacks for convenience –try not to eat too much, as you do not want anything stuck in your teeth during the interview.
    - o Eliminate loud conversations on your phone. If you must take a call before the interview, step outside. Otherwise, turn your phone off upon arrival.

- ✓ Eye contact

    - o Always look each interviewer in the eye when speaking.
    - o Never hold your head down.
    - o Even if an interviewer does not look at you, always give them your best attention.
    - o Shake hands with every interviewer on the panel upon leaving.

This is just brief preparation on how to present yourself for an interview. Remember that it is NEVER polite to be late, wear inappropriate clothing and act out of character. You are asking them to fund you for higher education, so prepare yourself by showing them that you want to go to school, and that you deserve the needed finances. If there is something you may be unsure of please go to your counselor for assistance.

Motivation Corner

From College to University

I remember a time in college when I was this ignorant sixteen year old. The teacher asked a class of about twenty to raise their hands if they plan on going to University. Eagerly, all but three lifted their hands into the air. I was one of the three. As my first year of college passed, so many ideas about my future went through my mind but I was always set on going into a job when I finished at eighteen. I even almost applied to join the Army once! That year soon had flown by, leaving me with two months of summer to dwell on my options; to think about what was really best, not just for me, but for the future of others too.

Throughout the first year, I gained a certain status of 'student teacher' relationship. I was known to spend all my spare time helping other students; whether it be at my college or the local high school down the road. My tutoring skills were the main reason I won 'Science and Math Student of the year'. As the summer passed, I thought more and more about what I really enjoyed, what I was good at, what I could do to help others in the future. Then, it hit me. Teaching. How would I do that? University.

The process of applying to University was lengthy and sometimes challenging, but I received an abundance of help from staff and current students. The second year of college was just a waiting game; waiting for that 'bing' on your phone to signify an email depicting whether or not you got that place you were after. The day finally came when the University of East Anglia, England offered me a place in their Science degree program! A mixture of feelings went through me all at once: fear, excitement, worry, happiness. All the same, simply, that was it. My life started there.

Two years on, things are different. I left the University of East Anglia, but I was not going to give up on my newly discovered dream. Instead I am now studying Bsc (Hons) Mathematics and it's learning with Open University; a distance learning University based in England. I am not going to say it's easy, because at times I wanted to give up but more than often I know that University is the best decision I made, for my future, my family's future and the future of others.

It's okay. You are allowed time. You are allowed time to consider your future and work out what it is that enlivens you. Don't just sit there tolerating your life; settle for what you desire.

Education has been and is currently a great tool. It has helped me gain and develop many essential life skills including problem solving, motivation and helping day-to-day decisions easier to make. Studying a Mathematics degree, I am a woman of statistics and statistics give many reasons as to why University education is a good choice (better salaries, more job satisfaction etc.). Statistics do not always tell the truth but I am going to say it loud and clear; this degree is changing my life. It is improving the quality of my life. It is helping me make decisions and it's educating me to provide a happy and successful future.

Emily Daniella Brown is a native of Norfolk, England. She is currently studying Bsc (Hons) Mathematics and it's learning with Open University, and has plans to graduate in July, 2018. Her career goal is to be a Math teacher.

The Importance of Mentors

*"Find someone to motivate you according
to your future, not your failures."*

There was a time when I first made it up in my mind that I wanted to continue pursuing my college degree. At the time, I was not sure how it was all going to happen, but I knew that I had to begin severing the dead people in my life so that I could move forward. After numerous attempts of going through the motions, allowing the negative people in my life to weigh me down, I finally gave up. I gave up on trying to do everything at once because I knew that it was impossible. During that time I sought out mentorships because I needed someone in my life to *motivate me according to my future, not my failures*. There were some good people in my life, but what I needed at the time was a mentor to push me to the next level. In the process of becoming a mentee, I learned how to mentor myself by speaking words of affirmation when I needed them the most. Ultimately, I was able to connect with positive people who knew the importance of sharing their life experiences to those wanting to make a change. This is how I began to grow and develop from the level of seeking to doing. Are there any dead relationships in your life you need to sever? Are there positive people in your life that can help mentor you along the way? If so, seek them and see how your life changes.

    Having a mentor is very important during this stage of your life. When it comes to seeking colleges and universities, as well as scholarships it can be overwhelming. There may be days you feel that your hard work is not paying off, and you cannot make it. Surrounding yourself around those who will encourage and provide you with the necessary resources for your development matters. In the end, you will be one step closer to your goal, and will have grown through the mentorship of someone who really cares. I encourage you today to believe in yourself no matter the obstacle, and to seek the good in everything and everyone regardless of how it appears.

Here are a few characteristics you would want to look for in a mentor:

1. Where are they at in their life?
2. How can they benefit you?
3. Are they knowledgeable about the goal you are trying to reach? If not, are they at least passionate about helping you move forward?
4. Are they committed to you as a mentor? If not, love them anyway, but you must keep going.

I have discovered the challenge with most of us is that we believe the word *no* before it is spoken. We take ownership over obstacle instead of seeing it as an opportunity to develop in the area you are lacking. The way we see vision in our mind is oftentimes the way we receive it. For example, if you see failure and trials constantly, you will begin to gravitate towards it. I would do this all the time –envision everything going wrong until it all goes wrong. This is a true definition of *Murphy's Law*, which basically tells us everything that could go wrong, will. Then I learned the characteristic of challenging challenge until it becomes an open door of opportunity. If you are honest with yourself, you will begin to see that there is a way to change what is wrong. This whole transformation you are going through by applying for colleges and scholarships is a great thing. Take the challenge seriously and do not allow those negative thoughts to get in your way.

I remember when I was going through the process of getting through school, and finding my way to pay for it. It seemed like there was always something going wrong, and I could not understand why. My personal finances had decreased tremendously, tuition fees began to increase, rent was always due, and bills were frustrated at me because I could not pay them. It got to a point where I knew my faith had to increase. My mind had to conceptualize that I was fully capable of completing the task at hand and getting through the unthinkable. My thought process changed, as well as my attitude towards the challenges that I was facing. I always speak these words to help propel me forward, *"I challenge change to build a mountain in front of me and watch as I climb it"*. In this moment, I challenge you to see yourself accomplishing your goals, envision yourself accepting a scholarship and walking across the stage, and I guarantee those thoughts will manifest fully in your life. What you think, you will become, so be careful of how you perceive yourself.

Seek mentors according to where you are in your life, and where you desire to go. Be patient with your mentor because they have a job to do, and keep them prayerful as they help to develop you forward.

Handling Rejection

*"Separate your fear from your dreams.
What's stopping you now?"*

It took me years to understand that I really deserved to go after my dreams and goals. I have always been a dreamer, but when you are brought up in a certain type of environment, and go to a certain type of school, you begin to feel the difference. Let me share something with you – I was always rejected as a child. My siblings always made fun of me and made me feel worthless, and then I would go to school and get bullied until I could not do anything but run into the restroom and cry my eyes out. I had few friends, and it seemed that I was always the one selected to be tormented. I was bullied. I was told that I was ugly. I was constantly laughed at. I was abused and overlooked. It had gotten to a point when I began to feel forgotten, and it took me a long time to snatch my mind back from the ridicule. It took many years of learning to believe in myself again, oftentimes having no one to turn to. I learned to be fearful of my dreams at a young age because it was forced into my head that I could not do it. When I came out of that mental distress, I had both hands up. I was ready to be arrested by success and destiny – better yet, I turned my own self in.

I know how you may feel when it comes to being rejected. You apply for a certain university and get a rejection letter. You apply for scholarships and was not selected as a recipient. You do not have many people around you who believe that you are capable of achieving your goals. You feel like it is too much, and quitting is the easiest thing to do. I challenge you to continue. The best piece of advice I can give you when it comes to rejection is that you already have everything inside of you to complete your journey.

Here is an exercise I started when rejection letters became too much. My remedy is a *Yes* Letter:

Dear Recipient:

This letter is to confirm that you have been selected as a super-natural recipient of favor. This letter is to certify that no matter what obstacle you go through; no matter how many no's you may hear; no matter how many times you've been challenged; no matter what road you are on now –you have been handpicked from a selection of many, to receive your heart's desire. There is nothing that no one can do to take this away from you. There is no struggle that can deter you from receiving.

The next steps you must follow clearly:

1. *Write down your goals.*
2. *Never stop believing.*
3. *If at first you do not succeed, try another way.*
4. *Have faith.*
5. *Be willing to receive.*

I would like to personally congratulate you on your accomplishment, for applying yourself and achieving what you set out to do. Welcome to the Kingdom of Scholars, for you have been inducted into the Alumni of Believers.

The point I am trying to make is that sometimes you have to encourage yourself. There were many times I did not have a mentor, or could not get hold of my counselors. There were some times when I felt like the road traveled was engulfing me into the struggle, and life itself was mocking me. I felt like I was running out of fuel and no matter which way I turned, I ended up at the same place, staring at the same wall, eating the same Top Ramen noodles. I kept telling myself that I could do this, but there were times when I would get that rejection letter in the mail and my thoughts would consume me. I understand how you may feel during this time, but what you have to remember is that it is a process. There are going to come times when you do not get the scholarship you applied for, or even get into the school you dreamed of.

This is why I stress the importance of not only applying for as many scholarships and schools as possible, but to envision yourself obtaining it. Sometimes our desires are but a fraction to what is really in store for us. At times we only have a limited view on what we desire because we are full of emotions and feelings. One day you want to be a doctor, but you are really passionate about being a dancer. Then you get frustrated when you do not get into medical school when in actuality your heart was never there. Sometimes we are rejected because it is an opportunity to see our mistakes and make them better the next go round.

There was one point in my life where I would get rejection after rejection. I started collecting my letters as fuel to drive me forward. I knew that someday, somebody would see my hard work and reward me for it. I still have the rejection letters to this day. Sometimes I look at them and remember that the rejection forced me to survive. I remember receiving one particular rejection letter during undergrad. The first thing I saw were those words we all dread to hear, "I regret to inform you that your application was not among those recommended for an award this year." By this time, I added that letter to my collection, and most importantly, I did not let it get me down. A few weeks later, I received this: "We are pleased to advise you on behalf of the (scholarship name here), that you have been awarded a scholarship of (amount here) to complete your education at a four-year institution." I was overjoyed. No matter what you do, always reapply and keep going.

Helpful Tip:

Rejection is like the cousin that shows up during the family reunion, but is never seen throughout the year. Rejection is only temporary, so quit making space for it in your closet when it comes around.

Recommendation Letters
No date

"Faith is standing behind me watching my back, while favor stands in front of me clearing my path. All things good shall come unto me, while all power manifest through me."

There are many things you have to submit when applying for colleges and/or scholarships, so it is better to prepare yourself ahead of time. A recommendation letter consists of a written statement from someone who is aware of your journey. It is very important to allow the person who is writing this for you adequate time to prepare. The last thing you need is a rushed job, which can count against you during the selection process. You need a great representation written boldly on a sheet of paper, declaring who you are by someone that values your choice of success. This letter should embody certain key points that you would like to be addressed. This is why you must communicate effectively when asking someone to do the letter for you.

    I remember when I was in undergrad and things were pretty hectic. I had to complete essay after essay, as well as submit numerous applications. This was a lot to do at one time. At this point, I began to get so overwhelmed that my recommendation letters took back seat to everything else. I asked one of my professors, who was actually the counselor over my department to do a recommendation letter for me. She agreed to help me, but what I failed to do at the time was ask her in advance, and schedule a meeting with her so that we could be on the same page with my goals. The end result in this letter was not good for me. Because of my lack of effort in being timely, my counselor wrote what she thought were my goals, and it turned out to be wrong information. I gladly accepted the letter because she did take the time to do it, but I did not actually use the letter because it did not properly represent who I was. This happened because I did not communicate the right information in a timely manner. It is very important that you take your time with this. If the scholarship application is due three months down the road, start immediately to prepare yourself. You want the best letter possible, and you want the deciding board to see and understand who you are from someone else's point of view.

Here are some steps to getting a great recommendation letter:

1. Become well acquainted with the teachers, faculty and staff at the school you are attending, or wanting to attend.
2. Have small talks with them about your goals.
3. Get the best grades possible. If for some reason you get a lower grade, talk with your teacher about how you can make it better. This shows commitment to your work.
4. Attend your teacher's office hours so that they will remember who you are.
5. Address your concerns of wanting to attend college and/or obtain a scholarship. Most teachers have valuable resources for students.
6. Ask questions when you do not understand something.
7. When the time comes to submit applications, those same teachers you've built a relationship with will be great candidates for writing your recommendation letter, and will enjoy doing it.
8. Always say thank you to the person who is writing the letter for you. They have committed their time to help you out.
9. Give them an update with the process on how everything is going.
10. Back yourself up by getting multiple recommendation letters in a separate sealed, signed envelope. You will be happy that you did.

Sample Recommendation Letters
(used by permission)

Sample #1

Dear Selection Panel:

I am writing this letter to support Toi Nichelle in her efforts to attend School. Toi Nichelle is an incredible creative writer, a person of the highest caliber, and an innovative and emerging voice in the creative arts. Ms. Nichelle is developing into a well-rounded student and possesses extraordinary dedication and integrity. In recent years, she has been dedicated to bringing up her grades and keeping her academic record strong. I hope that you will consider her for future study in your program.

I have known Ms. Nichelle for about 1 year, and I served as her Creative Reading & Writing instructor at San Francisco State University last fall. In this undergraduate creative writing class, I was struck by the vulnerability and depth that Toi Nichelle brought to her writing. She took every assignment as an opportunity to deeply explore life and language's potential in the greater society. Her critical questions inspire others to look closely at the world and to wake up to the richness of being alive at this time and in this place. She is a skilled writer, one whose work is both honest and moving; she freely intertwines her own brand of critical inquiry with the tender and relevant aspects of being human. Her writing spans vast terrain from politics to aesthetics and from nature to relationships and was consistently in the top 15% of the creative writing class. Everything is fair game in her work, which requires much of the reader and delivers in equal or greater measure.

Within the writing class, Toi Nichelle was revered for not only her admirable productivity, but also for the power and clarity of her undertakings. She is a wonderful writer and inspired reader. She has considerable presence for a young author, which is undoubtedly due to her varied life experiences and the fullness with which she approaches any given task. I am certain that her studies would only deepen her work, allowing her to explore the arts in more depth and continue to write and publish extensively; again, I am certain that in the midst of all this activity, she will remain remarkably self-directed in terms of her creative and scholarly work. She's the "real thing."

Beyond her tremendous talent and generosity, Ms. Nichelle is a noble human being. She is well liked by peers and friends and will surely make the most of her studies. As the former director of Small Press Traffic Literary Arts Center at the California College of the Arts, I have worked with countless young writers and Ms. Nichelle stands out as one of the most promising among them. Toi Nichelle is an excellent candidate for study, one that any learning community would undoubtedly be richer for including. Ms. Nichelle will prove a wonderful addition to your program. Please feel free to contact me should you need further information.

    Sincerely yours,

    (Name left out)

Sample #2

To Whom It May Concern:

I am writing in support of Toi Nichelle. She was my student during spring semester 2012, and she also worked for me as an intern at The Poetry Center, a program within the Creative Writing Department at San Francisco State University, where she focused on social media in support of our public programs: a weekly series of events featuring distinguished guest writers.

Regarding her work as a student, Toi is very self-motivated and dedicated to her scholarship. She brought a high level of maturity, seriousness of endeavor, and generosity into the classroom environment, and had a welcome effect on other students. Everyone benefited by her presence and participation. As my social media intern, she was reliable, thoughtful when comprehending the history and complexity of our programs (we present 30-50 contemporary writers in public programs each year), and the particular milieu of the organization and field. At the same time she brought in fresh ideas, worked well to realize the goals we agreed on, and was remarkably reliable.

On a personal level, we shared an interest in classic gospel music (I teach classes, as Adjunct Professor at California College of the Arts, in music and literature, with emphasis on African American traditions), and it's been a real pleasure for me to compare notes with her, as she is active in that area and she knows a good deal of the history of the music.

All in all, I'm impressed by what she has done during her time at San Francisco State University, and am confident that she'll bring the same qualities and practices to her future work. I recognize that the kind of social and cultural goals that are close to her heart are valuable, and would argue that any organization would benefit by the presence of participants with strong connections to community in the work they are doing. I've seen comparable students go on to do remarkable and innovative work, e.g., with young people, whether in the teaching field or in social oriented organizations, and I know there are many directions one can undertake while making strong use of their studies as a writer.

Please do contact me with any questions.

Sincerely,

Steven Dickison
Director, The Poetry Center and American Poetry Archives
Lecturer, Department of Creative Writing

Sample #3

To Whom It May Concern:

I am pleased to write a letter of recommendation on behalf of Toi Nichelle. Toi worked as a social media intern at San Francisco State University's Poetry Center and American Poetry Archives during Spring Semester 2012. Toi has demonstrated initiative, purpose and follow-through in all the tasks assigned to her. When we asked her to work in the area of social media, promoting Poetry Center events via Twitter –she came up with the idea to tweet quotes of African-American poets during African-American history month. Shen then expanded that idea to add video clips and biographical information to introduce these poets to new readers.

Toi's interpersonal communication skills are strong –and she put them to good use on our behalf. This is a relatively new internship position, and we appreciated the energy and enthusiasm that Toi brought to it. Unafraid to jump in and offer her ideas, she is also good at listening and refining her approach in response to feedback. The internship opportunity has provided her with hands-on experience working behind the scenes with a small literary arts organization using social media for audience development. We were very grateful for her assistance. I am happy to give her my strong recommendation.

    Please feel free to contact me with any questions.
    Sincerely,
    (Name left out)

Sample #4

To Whom It May Concern:

I am writing in support of Toi Nichelle as a candidate for an Associate Students Scholarship for the College of Humanities, now called Arts and Humanities.

As an advisor of Toi's for several years, I know that she is a hard-working Creative Writing major, Africana Studies minor, with a wealth of personal experience and insight that speaks well for the ability to endure the most desperate of circumstances and to prosper from her adversity. Raised by a single mother and homeless while a young woman in Los Angeles, Toi Nichelle has profited from that experience by enrolling at our university, where she maintains a 3.45 average, and has turned the insights she gained from her own struggle to aiding troubled teenagers through church-run programs in Pittsburg, California. She works on verbal communication with youth through their Literacy Programs, as well as working hard to achieve good grades and be a responsible member of the SFSU community.

I am also aware that she is applying to the international Studies Program here and hopes to spend time in Ghana, learning their culture and language. This would be a wonderful, life-expanding opportunity for her and illustrates her courage and insight in seeking out opportunities beyond her comfort zone and in territories that will expand her humanly and intellectually.

I am therefore pleased to recommend a young woman who hasn't been harmed by life's adversities and the difficulties of a complex and unhappy childhood but strengthened and renewed. As a writer, a student, and a human being, I am deeply moved by Toi Nichelle and her struggles and hope that you will see fit to grant her this opportunity for scholarship support.

    Sincerely,
    (Name left out)

Sample #5

To Whom It May Concern:

This letter is written in support of my student, Toi Nichelle, who is applying for a Kennedy-King Memorial Fund Scholarship. In my 26 year tenure at the community college, currently serving as History Program Coordinator, I have enjoyed working relationships with a variety of students, a few among them being persons of unusual distinction and promise. Toi Nichelle is one of these beyond all telling. In fact of the many dozens of letters of reference I have written over the years, I cannot remember a time when my expression of support for a student was as deeply felt as in this instance. As an "older" continuing student struggling valiantly to overcome an earlier life of heart-breaking setbacks and bitter personal torment, the kind of obstruction that would ruin the lives of most of us, Toi has emerged as a gallant exemplar of the passion for learning that we teachers too seldom find among so many others under our charge. Toi is a warm, gracious, engaging and quietly patient person to know, and her disciplined, alert, caring approach to study renders her an unforgettable presence in any classroom. Born to learn her highly literate and expressive way of handling ideas and fearless grappling with complex and demanding topics of human import makes her a valuable resource in the educational process. Since I have known Toi from my Fall semester course in Ancient World History, and (unknown to her) have compared notes with other instructor colleagues equally impressed with her aptitude and diligence in other course settings, I can readily affirm her capacity for advanced university work, and the appropriateness of her aim to prepare for a professional career in Language Arts and Creative Writing. On a personal note, as one who once marched with Martin Luther King, and was active in the Robert F. Kennedy Campaign for President, I must assert that if any student fully manifests the deepest intent of the Kennedy-King Scholarship Award, that student would be Toi Nichelle.

It should be understood that the Ancient World History course Toi and I shared last semester (as with all courses under my instruction) functions to serve students who will seek advanced degrees in the CSU/UC State systems. The course has a reputation for rigor beyond the community college norm. I personally supervised Toi through all phases of classwork, including graded demonstration of her reading, writing, speaking, research team and analysis skills, and found her to be consistently superior among very able peers. Toi has cultivated a posture of mature diligence, one who accepts criticism with grace and responds enthusiastically to the challenge of new ideas in a socially diverse environment. Toi works fruitfully with others while maintaining a habit of thoughtfulness and clear purpose encouraging others to do likewise. Toi, already a published poet and admired writer, will thrive in a university culture where skilled accomplishment really matters and where professional commitment to learning is steady and unflinching. It is Toi's hope to advance her creative writing career in notable academic programs (perhaps San Francisco State or California State East Bay) where the inevitable ordeal of gaining a sustainable "publication signature" is honestly prepared for.

Toi's current posture of classroom competence and quiet dignity easily conceals the harsh circumstances of her past, the story of which I, as her instructor, have only glimpsed in her telling. Once neglected, abused and homeless, leading to suicidal episodes as a young woman, Toi knows too well the demons of despair. Having now secured her soul's foundation in faithful, thoughtful literary expression, Toi has found the resources to live a life of creative purpose that will inspire all who are touched by her charismatic spirit. For the Kennedy-King Scholarship committee to favor her now with financial means to continue her educational advancement, will, I believe, find all who know her well-pleased with her promising future of meaningful human services.

    Respectfully yours,
    (Name left out)

Sample #6

To whom it may concern:

I have known Toi Nichelle for a year and a half. Toi was an excellent student in my English/Creative Writing class. I was so impressed with her talent, her intelligence and her person that I went out of my way to get to know her personally in my office hours (besides learning a great deal about her from her talented writing).

Let me say from the outset that Toi is one of the most outstanding students that I have had the privilege to work with in my 20 years of teaching. And this is not only because of her academic potential which, as I said above, knows no limits. It is her character that is amazing.

When I think of Toi the following words describe my appreciation and understanding of her –character, initiative, persistence, strong work ethic, inspiring values, and someone who will make a difference in this world.

First of all, you must understand that Toi grew up in Los Angeles, and by the time she was 14, her mother had lost her job, and they were homeless and living out of a grey Corsica. Toi never let anyone in high school know and just wore the same thing to school every day until it was no longer wearable. By the time she was fifteen, her mother basically abandoned her, it seemed, and she ate where she could, did her homework at school, stayed for long periods of time at a friend's house, and learned to walk for hours. At one point, she slept on a park slide. She was able to graduate from high school. At the age of 19, she got a job and worked her way up from cashier to manager. She has been involved with church since she was a teenager and it has kept her steady. She has always done volunteer work in whatever church she has belonged to and was soon able to get a small, very run-down apartment in Los Angeles. She learned to walk everywhere and one of my favorite stories that illustrates Toi's amazing persistence and work ethic is that as a manager of the warehouse she worked for, she would close the store at 11 p.m. and it would take her two hours to walk home because she didn't own a car. She would turn around and walk back at 3 a.m. so she could open the door by 5 a.m. She didn't complain, she did her work and she educated herself, taking classes at a local community college. She had begun writing poetry as a teenager and by the time she was in her early twenties, she self-published her first book of poems, "Mirror to my Soul" which she convinced local bookstores to sell. Since that time she has written a second book and helped other writers publish.

Secondly, you must also understand that even though she lived on the streets for a number of years because of her incredible values, she did not get involved with drugs or prostitution etc. When I asked her how in the world she kept herself safe, she said, "I learned to run fast! And I walked and walked and walked. And I found a church."

A reader since childhood, Toi has in many ways educated herself. When she came to Los Medanos (and is now so close to transferring), it took her a while to adjust to the structure of college and get the high grades she is so capable of getting. Her current GPA represents so much persistence, hard work, and frankly, smarts. When she was in elementary and middle school, before things fell apart in her family, she was in the magnet program, which is an accelerated program for very bright students.

Today, Toi is a lovely strong hard working and extremely intelligent young lady. She works part-time, goes to school full-time, and rents a small room. She attends a local church where she currently is teaching a volunteer poetry course. Toi has recently been accepted into the prestigious creative writing program at SF State University for a B.A. in Creative Writing. I believe in Toi's dream –she will graduate from there with flying colors, she will get her M.A. and she will become a marvelous, insightful and inspiriting teacher. Toi quite simply believes in a greater purpose than just 'making it', she wants to give back and I, for one, know that she will.

Professor, English
Los Medanos College
(Name left out)

Helpful Tip:

Always ask the person who is writing your recommendation letter to not include a date. You want to be able to reuse it over and over again.

Motivation Corner

Education is Priceless

There is a great deal of pressure around preparing for college. There are tests, applications, grades, and most importantly financial aid that have to be in order before embarking on a journey to campus. I worked very hard throughout high school to excel academically with the hopes it would create more opportunity for me after high school.

I was blessed enough to be accepted to every school I applied to. I graduated an honor student. My GPA was most competitive. I was on track to obtain a degree from a prestigious college and pursue the career of my dreams. Until reality hit! I had to face the fact that I did not have the funds to attend any of the schools I had applied to; a high school graduate with no income. My only options were either skip college and join the workforce, defer college until I could afford it, or sign up for student loans.

Of course I applied for FAFSA which essentially helped generate funds and financial opportunity for me, but my fear still remained. I did not want to rack up student loans and begin a life accruing uncontrollable debt. So I turned to scholarships. Applying for scholarships became my newest hobby. I would spend every free moment searching and applying.

Unlike most students, I was very lonely in college. Working two jobs, taking a full course load, and studying did not allow much time to make a lot of friends. Although my school was only an hour away from my family, my church, and my friends back home, I did not have a car to go see them. There were many times where I would feel overwhelmed and doubt my decision to attend college. I felt it would be so much easier to go just back home. But then I remembered how hard I worked my entire life to get to college. To get to a college of my choosing. I reminded myself of my goals. I refocused my attention on the task at hand which was to graduate college and begin a career.

Eventually, I resolved the issue of loneliness by finding a bus that could take me downtown to the train station. I saved money and took the train at least once a month to go see my family. I also joined a few clubs on campus including study groups. This allowed me to make friends.

It's true what they say in life –what you put in determines what you get out. I received several scholarships and grants that provided me enough money to attend the school of my choice. And because of hard work and determination, I am a UC Riverside Alumni with a Bachelor of Science degree in Business Administration with a concentration in accounting.

College was a struggle. I worked two jobs and maintained full-time student status. I also had to take out a few small student loans. But the experience and knowledge I gained in college was well worth it. To me, my college education was an investment. In today's times, it is not enough to just have a high school diploma. To be competitive in the market requires a minimum of a bachelor's degree.

The moral of the story: education is priceless. It's the one asset that guarantees you a future. There are resources out there to make college affordable for everyone. But the money is not going to fall in your lap. You have to be proactive and pursue those funds. Because again, what you put in will determine what you get out.

College will be hard work. Everyone will struggle in a different way. My advice for dealing with tough times is RRR:

- Refocus on the task at hand, that is, to complete college and begin a professional career of your choice.
- Remind yourself of how hard you worked to get to where you are. Encourage yourself to keep going.
- Resolve the issue. Find a compromise that will make the situation easier on you. Quitting is not a resolution and should not be an option.

Enjoy the experience but remember to take it serious. It is up to you to take advantage of the opportunities of this journey. Make sure you network; meet new people and make professional connections. There are times where what you know will not get you in the door but who you know may hold the door of opportunity open for you.

Take advantage of internships and opportunities to gain experience. Most employers require experience and a degree. College is the best place to earn both.

Be competitive. Absorb the information you learn and apply it to the career you intend to seek. You and all of your classmates will most likely enter the workforce at the same time. When employers see your résumé you want them to see more than just the bachelor's degree you obtained. Experience and skill development are treasures on this journey. Make sure you don't miss out.

Be open minded. I went into college not knowing what career path I wanted to take. Then I chose psychology. Then sociology. Then I wanted to be a teacher. Then an engineer. Then a lawyer. Until finally I decided that I want to be an accountant. As you learn, your career ambitions may change, but that's normal. Each course you take will likely teach you something new about yourself and generate new ideas for you. Follow those ideas and be open to explore educationally.

Rashauna R. Smallwood is a bright and intelligent young lady, residing in Henderson, NV. She received her Bachelor of Science degree in Business Administration with a concentration in accounting from UC Riverside. She is the product of hard work and perseverance, and encourages all young students to go after their dreams.

Thank You Letters

*"Don't ever let anyone justify your abilities,
for you do not know all that you're capable of."*

Have you ever felt that warm tingly feeling inside your belly when someone gave you a card? Maybe it was a birthday card. Get well soon card. My condolences card. No matter what day it was, getting a card from someone shows that they care and are thinking of you. This is the same when you give someone a thank you card, which may also be in the form of a letter. Personally, I chose to write thank you letters because I enjoy the craft of writing and I understand the significance of words.

After you have done the work and have received the scholarship, go the extra mile by sending out a thank you card/letter to the committee, or school staff that were involved in the decision process. It is important to make sure you keep that connection with those who have helped you along the way. They were the bridge between a dream and your reality, and it should never go unnoticed. You will be happy you kept the connection going in the future when you need help getting into Graduate school, or when you may need a reference for the new career move your degree will bring.

On the next page, I have written a sample thank you letter I used during my time in undergrad. Please keep in mind that I shared my story in the letter during the time it happened, so make sure you share your own personal story, if you choose to write a letter. Be specific. Take your sponsor on a journey, allowing them to feel included in your process. The worst thing you can do to your sponsor is to not include them. What you have to remember is that they were the ones that believed in you when many failed to. They supported you financially, and it makes a world of difference in your academic costs. Be kind to them, often reaching out to give an update on your academics and graduation ceremony. It is also good to extend an invitation to them during your graduation. You'll be surprised at the responses that will come your way.

Sample Thank You Letter

Honored Sponsor:

This past fall (2012), I journeyed away on an 18-hour flight to another country in the United Kingdom. I was so excited because I had the opportunity to actually see some of the things I could only dream of growing up. You helped make this possible for me. When I first stepped foot on the plane my heart was over-joyed with tears because here I was –this young girl who grew up in some of the worst parts of Los Angeles –sitting on a plane traveling to some foreign land that I would call home for nine months. I did not know what to expect when I boarded the plane, but I knew that no matter what I encountered, God would be right there with me.

It was my first long flight I had ever taken in my life and when I reached my mid-destination in Philadelphia, I felt at ease. I roamed throughout the airport, waiting for my two hour lay-over to pass, and met a nice woman who was headed back home to Africa. I was excited because we got to talking and she pushed my desire to the limit in wanting to visit Africa one day. Who knows what God has in store for me? As the plane began to rise and turbulence kicked in, the lady who I met earlier gripped the sides of her seat and started explaining to me her fear of the rocky movements the plane was experiencing. I sat back with eager attention to listen, though in my mind I felt at peace in the arms of God. I was amazed because I thought that I would have been the one having panic attacks while some thousand feet up in the air. I was calm and my spirit was settled.

There were some challenges that I had to face once I departed from the plane. It was definitely a moment of surrender for me, and the unexpected situations that happened cost me financially, and pushed me to the edge a bit; although when I look back on what happened, I feel that it strengthened me more. Why am I saying all of this? It is because the seed you sowed into my life was the cushion that helped me to make it to my final destination across the water to England. If I did not have the cushion (seed) you planted into my life at that moment, the little girl inside of me probably would not have known what to do. In saying this, I have to say THANK YOU! I know that I have said it many times before, but your seed was a life-saver at the time I needed it the most, and I am forever grateful for your obedience and sacrifice in taking a chance on someone like myself. Believe me when I say that my prayers are graced with mere gratitude.

After everything, I am continuing to push harder in the coming semester, which I will be departing from England at the end of May to participate in my commencement ceremony at San Francisco State University. One thing I do know is that I am almost done –can see the finish line right in front of me. I will definitely keep you posted on my final semester here in England, but in the meantime –thank you.

Helpful Tip:

It does not have to be a traditional thank you letter. Be yourself, share your story. Write as much as you wish, or as little as you like. Just DO NOT forget the words –THANK YOU!

"In school I did not always get the *A* I wanted,
but I got the *B* that I deserved.
Therefore, I have learned to see the growth
I need to take that extra mile down the
road called *better.*"

Study Abroad

United Kingdom: Norwich, England
(My journey)

Study Abroad Experience
Passports, Visas, Clearance Forms

> Please be advised. The information listed is for studying in the United Kingdom and may not apply to studying in other countries. This is just a brief description of my experience, which can provide basic answers to your study abroad questions.

One of the greatest things you can do in school is visit another country. It does not matter if it is a short visit, or for an academic year. Being that college is a time when you discover yourself, grow as an individual and connect with various people from around the globe, why not see what the world looks like from the lens of a different culture? I decided to study abroad in the United Kingdom during my senior year because I wanted to experience something different. Most of my time in school was spent in classrooms and working side jobs to get by, so I needed to have a greater experience before I walked the stage that following year. When I finally made it up in my mind, I had to begin positioning myself all over again for scholarships, housing, airfare etc. It was a huge challenge, but well worth the sacrifice.

Below, I have listed various information for those who want to travel outside of their own country to study. When reading, please remember that every country is different and may require additional information, but the basic information is the same. The facts listed are to assist those who are seeking for advice on studying abroad before making the decision. It is also useful information for those who have made the decision, and need help on where to start and what to expect.

The information that I will provide will consist of departure preparations, flight information, arrival procedures, packing, living/residency, campus description, academics, transportation, food, entertainment, college affairs and course curriculum. Cumulatively these topics will provide you a thorough comparison on living in the United States versus life in the United Kingdom. In my approach, I hope to give you the best information possible so that every applicant has a successful experience. Please check with the school you will be attending to view the information pertaining to that country. Here is what you need to know to prepare for your arrival in your host country:

- ✓ Departure Preparations
- ✓ Climate
- ✓ Packing
- ✓ Flight information
- ✓ Arrival rules and regulations
- ✓ Grading Scale
- ✓ Housing
- ✓ Academics
- ✓ Campus life/Social life
- ✓ Food
- ✓ Course Curriculum
- ✓ Religion
- ✓ Gender/Sexuality/Culture
- ✓ Shopping/Leisure/Entertainment/Transportation
- ✓ Travel

Departure Preparations

There is a lot to be done when preparing to leave the country for any amount of time. If you are anything like me, you will be trying your best to get multiple scholarships to help fund not only your time abroad, but also any additional travel expenses that could pop up. The first step I had to take was getting a passport, which I suggest getting done ahead of time as there may be complications that will delay your passport's arrival. In the midst of getting my passport, I was also filling out the necessary forms for my visa and multiple essays for study abroad scholarships, so my time was well spent in preparing.

If I could have done anything differently, it would be to make sure that I gave myself enough time to complete each important task. It can be very stressful filling out foreign forms and waiting what seems like ages for a response.

Climate

The weather was not that bad when I first arrived in England in September 2011. It was not too cold around that time, but a few weeks later it began to get really cold. The winds can be heavy, as well as when it rains and snows. By the way, the snow is very intense if you are not used to this type of weather condition. The British culture seems very comfortable with the snow. There were always people walking around in the snow wearing thin tights and mini-skirts with sandals. I could not believe it because I had on thick layers of leggings, jeans, a scarf, a hat and gloves.

For the academic year, you only experience the fall/winter and spring, both of these seasons can be intensely cold. Prepare yourself.

Packing

If you are planning to study in England, I suggest you pack multiple pairs of jeans/leggings (for girls), thermo under garments, thick scarves that can cover your face when needed, thick leather gloves, hats and the best umbrella you could possibly find. You will want to pack light for travel, so you might want to purchase some of these things in the city when you arrive, but just keep in mind that it is more expensive in the pound currency for that country. Also, do not forget to bring some good boots that will last throughout your stay there. You will thank me in the end.

Flight Information

Check your flight tickets to make sure that you are flying into Norwich, England or whatever country you are studying in. When I first arrived in Amsterdam, I became aware that I did not have a connecting flight into Norwich from Amsterdam, which left me stranded with two large luggage and carry-on bags. I was able to purchase an extra ticket for my connecting flight into Norwich, but because it was last minute the price was very expensive, which was not helpful for a first experience into another country. You can avoid this type of difficulty by CHECKING your flight tickets before you leave. Don't say I did not warn you.

    I departed from San Francisco airport on US Airways, and had a connecting flight in Philadelphia on British Airways. The baggage fees were not as expensive, as the first bag (no more than 50 lbs.) was free, and I was charged a $100 fee for the second bag. You do not have to collect your baggage in Philadelphia or whatever connecting state your flight lands in from the United States. You just pick your baggage up at your final destination.

    One thing you should be aware of is that after you have completed your program and are returning home to the United States, you have to pick up your luggage from the connecting state you land in, go through customs, re-check your luggage in, and go through security once more. Yes, this was a pain, especially if you have multiple luggage to claim, but when you are returning from a foreign country they want to double-check everything about you before you re-enter the country.

Arrival/Rules and Regulations

If you study at the University of East Anglia, and fly into NORWICH, then they will have shuttle buses picking up students from the airport and bringing them to the university. The welcoming committee will be wearing UEA shirts. Once you arrive at orientation you will have to go to the LCR (Lower Common Room) building to check in. Have your passport on hand, so that they can scan it in the system. Also, be prepared to receive emails on getting your passport scanned every semester for security reasons. They want to make sure that your visa is still good and you are on track. In the LCR, you will pick up your room keys, if you are staying on campus, your ID campus card (which lets you into the 24-hour library), and information on the group orientation. Pay attention to all the volunteers with the UEA shirts, as they will be looking to see who needs a ride on the shuttle bus to their accommodation. If you are like me and arrived at 10pm, then the shuttle is very helpful when you have lots of luggage. This is a NO CHARGE service to all international students. If you are not living somewhere on campus, then the best thing I can tell you is to arrive to the campus during the day, and there will be local buses going throughout the city. You can take your luggage on board to get to your living destination. The price is 2.70 for the young person's discount (two-way), and 4.00 (for regular fair). For the young person's discount you have to be 25 and under, but they never really check. Just ask for a young person's discount and it'll be okay, as well as save you money.

The next day, you'll have a group orientation where the staff will share what to expect in their country and on campus. For instance, the British way of saying hello is, "you alright"? The proper way to respond is to say it back to them. Also, the grading system is very different from the United States. If you get a 60% on a test or paper, DO NOT be alarmed. A 60% is basically a *B-B+* average, although here in the States that is almost a failing grade. If you get a 70% then you are one of their best students. It just means you got an *A*.

The best way to set up a bank account is to go to the bank on campus, which is Barclay's. The first few weeks can be extremely busy, as there are lines (queue –this is how they say line) of students wanting to open a bank account. Once you get in front of the line, be prepared to show your campus ID/passport, proof of accommodation (which will basically be the paper given to you when you received your keys) and whatever else they ask for. It is a real easy process in opening an account. If you wish to keep your personal account from back home like myself, it is easy to do a foreign transfer. Barclay's do not charge, but you should check with your personal bank to see the fees that apply. I bank with Chase, and when I did a transfer into my student account at Barclay's bank, Chase charged about a $40 one-time fee, so make sure you transfer enough for that one semester. I kept my account back home for personal reasons, and because I was returning home the following year, so it worked out for me in the end. Barclay's will also send you letters with your secure pin to activate your student account, so keep on the lookout for those. For students staying on campus, you can pick up all mail at the campus Post Room, located right below the Arts building. Just show your ID, tell them what accommodation you are staying at, and they will give you your mail. Off campus students will not be able to pick up mail on campus, but every student can send mail on campus at the Post Office to anywhere in the world. The fees are expensive, but the service is there, so you won't have to go into the city to do this.

Obtaining a cell phone is easy as setting up a bank account. Just go into the city, and purchase a phone of your choice. I suggest that you get the cheapest phone possible. I paid around 10 pounds for my phone. I also suggest that you use it for emergencies ONLY, as it can be very expensive topping up your phone credits, which can be done at the ATM machine on campus. Personal calls can be done from a FREE Skype account (skype.com). This is truly the easiest way to stay in touch back home in your country, and does not really cost, unless you purchase a subscription, which is around $19 every three months.

Housing

I stayed in the University Village, which is divided into undergrad and post-grad. My first semester there was just okay, only because I was stuck with all first year students who were very loud and not used to cleaning up after themselves. The kitchen was always dirty, filled with dishes in the sink, and they were always drinking and having parties. Because I am not a first year student, and my focus was to study, meet new people and have some type of peace and quiet, I eventually moved out into the post-grad dorms. This was much better for me, and I was surrounded by all Asian and Chinese students. They are very communal and quiet to say the least, so if you do not enjoy all the loud noise and parties, you can request to be in the postgrad rooms. It will save you the trouble in doing this early.

Academics

The first thing I would say is that you make sure you have all the classes needed for your major. Reason being is that when I arrived classes were all over the place, and a lot of exchange students were running around trying to get the right classes they needed. Don't get me wrong, it will not be as difficult to get the classes needed, but at least have some idea. Keep in mind that some courses go from one semester to the next, which in some cases, if you take a class in the fall, when you return you will have to take the exam for it. For example, if you are taking business or law courses for the fall, your exam may be given in the spring. It all depends on the major and courses you take.

To my understanding, this gives students an opportunity to study over break and prepare for the final exam. Hope this makes sense. Not all classes are like this, but it's good to know. The academic structure set up here is completely different from the United States. For instance, when you complete papers you will have to submit them online to the 'hub', not the teacher. Also, most classes have the lecture with an attached seminar, so most classes can last between 3-4 hours, depending.

I will not lie, I have had some not so good experiences with some of the staff and professors here, but overall the majority of the people are really nice. If you ever feel uncomfortable, your personal advisor is there to listen. I've used him many times. Other than that, it's a good school and it's a good choice nonetheless.

Campus Live/Social Life

Do not expect to see a lot of school spirit with cheers and dances, but they do have social mixers for the students, club nights in the blue bar, and designated international trips where they take you out to see the castles, mansions, cobble-stone streets, boat rides to see the seals, and Cambridge. Purchase your tickets in advance, as they do sell out quickly. If you decide to do the Seal Boat Sail Trip, try and see if they have another one in the spring. The one that takes place in the fall can have adverse weather conditions. Luckily I did not go in the fall because it poured down raining on all the students while they were on a boat looking at the seals. The boat is open, so there is no covering. I went to the one in the spring, and although it was cold, it did not rain. I felt so sorry for those who went in December.

Food

If you are used to American food with the rich spices and blends of flavor, then prepare yourself for the blandness of British food. They have lots of pre-packaged sandwiches (no matter where you go), coffees (yes, they do have Starbucks), teas etc. You can shop at your local Tesco's, which everyone does, or Morrison's in the city. Either way, you have an opportunity to make your own food and save some money. Overall, the food is very bland, so prepare your taste buds for that. It is also good to receive care packages from home with dry foods from your culture to implement into their culture, as I have. You will notice different brands on everything and different fast food places, except for McDonald's and Burger King.

Course curriculum

The course curriculum will take a bit of adjusting to. Everything is basically done in the HUB, located in the Arts building. You submit coursework online through their portal to the HUB, which they will then print it out and submit it to your tutor (they are rarely called professors); then weeks later you will be notified by email that your coursework is available in the HUB to be picked up from the pigeon holes in the Arts building. If you have trouble finding your pigeon hole, just go to the front desk at the HUB and they will point you in the right direction. They really do try and help.

It can also be very difficult to talk to your professor about your work in person, even during their office hours. My suggestion would be to email them with the situation first, then make an appointment with them. Once you get in front of them they already know the situation so the meeting is just to clarify and correct the problem. If you do not get the grade you think you deserve, you can petition that your work be re-evaluated, which you will have to fill out a form, and wait for a response.

Religion

There are different faiths and religions on campus, which can be very interesting to learn. Because I am a Christian, I looked into those groups on campus that practice my faith and connected with them. If you have a different faith, go online to the UEA website, or go to their Chaplaincy building on campus and search the different groups that hold meetings. The majority of the time you will discover groups that are actively serving in their faith right on campus. For those of Christian faith, there is a group called *Signature* on campus that meet to have bible study and fellowship. They also have drama meetings where they practice to put on Christian plays, choir practice for those who like to sing and one-on-one meetings just to get together and have outings. On Sundays, they all meet up with one another and walk up to the church (not too far from campus) for a worship service. You will enjoy their company.

Additional Advice

Be yourself! What I have discovered in my time abroad is that they are accepting of all types of genders and sexuality. Because I am of the African American race, my experience was different in the sense of being around other cultures and races in another country. At first, it was hard to fit in, but then I realized that it was impossible to fit in. I learned to be myself and because of that people accepted me for who I am. The British culture was more interested in my American lifestyle, which allowed me to truly be who I was made to be.

I can say that you will not see a lot of African American students studying abroad in the United Kingdom. I was really the only student of my culture there, which pushed me to adapt to a whole different atmosphere. It was actually very interesting to see how different my culture was to the great people of England.

Shopping/Leisure/Entertainment/Transportation

If you are looking for things to do outside of the campus on your own, the city center is about a 35 minute bus ride. You'll find shops, malls, food places, theatre's etc. Also, everyone will fall in love with your different accent. Since I am American everyone kept saying that I have an amazing accent, which baffles me because they are the ones who sound different (at least to Americans). The buses 25/35/35A leave from the campus and go into the city center. I believe they run well into the early hours of the morning, so it's okay if you stay out late and socialize with friends.

Travel

There are plenty of opportunities for you to travel throughout England, visiting castles etc., and also going to other countries like France or Italy, which I had the pleasure of touring. Campus life here is different than San Francisco State as well. Let's just say they like to party hard at night at the campus pub, but during the day it's mostly all about studying. There will be many opportunities to travel with groups on campus (do join the travel society, they are on Facebook). The Dean of Students office (DOS) are always planning tours for international students only, so just pay attention to the bulletins they send out through email. It is an awesome way to tour through England, get into London and meet new international friends. The Norwich train is also a good quick way to get into London. Also, Megabus and National Express are both good bus services that students use to travel into different parts of England, and other countries. Both of these services leave from the campus, so it is very convenient and inexpensive. Go to megabus.com or nationalexpress.com for more information. I used both of these services when I went into Paris, Italy and Amsterdam. Safe travels!

Travels in: England, Paris and Italy!

Here are some questions that may be asked when writing an essay to study abroad:

- ✓ What are some of your personal, professional and academic goals?
- ✓ How do you believe these goals will affect or help your study abroad experience?
- ✓ How have you prepared yourself for the study abroad experience? Met with counselors?
- ✓ What personal experiences have equipped you to study abroad?
- ✓ If interested, what are some activities you desire to explore while studying abroad? Campus Clubs?
- ✓ Have you held any leadership roles? If not, are you seeking to be part of a leadership team while abroad?
- ✓ Please explain any deficiencies noted on your application. What were those circumstances? How have they helped you to move forward?

THE RESULT

"I have learned to take challenge as a seed offering, like that of a tree. In time, my dream will grow."

The result is simple. It is the outcome of your hard work over the years and months of preparation. After you have dedicated yourself to succeeding and accomplishing your academic goals, you will begin to see things line up in a way that you've never imagined. I started out wanting to obtain my A.A. degree, get a job and as long as my bills were paid, I would be okay. The one thing that propelled me forward is that there were other desires hidden inside of me that would not let me stop there. I continued to push myself and soon received my B.A. degree, studied in the United Kingdom, traveled throughout Europe and developed a boast of confidence that keeps me going to this day. Everything I mentioned above was paid for by scholarships, grants, sponsorships and so forth. I really did not have to come out of pocket for my academic fees because I took the initiative to go further. When it got to the point that my study abroad experiences were completely paid for, I was in total awe. It all started with a mere thought, and the actions I took to better myself, while seeking greater opportunity.

As we go into a close of this book, I want to ask you a few questions:

1. Do you have a better understanding on how to start the process of applying for scholarships/schools?
2. Have you made it clear the field you desire to go in?
3. Have you set up meetings with your current counselors? If not, do it now.
4. Have you toured the college/university you would like to attend?
5. Have you searched for scholarships that pertain to your field?
6. Have you figured out what category you are in when selecting a scholarship? (Academic or Financial Need Base).

7. Have you sought out great mentors to help you along the way?
8. Have you begun to write your essay? If you made it this far in the book, you should already have a draft, so start now.
9. Have you figured out the cost of tuition it will take to attend the college/university of your choice?
10. Have you sought out sponsorships by writing a letter and mailing them off?
11. If you are in high school, have you talked to your counselor? If not, now is the time to do so.
12. If current/returning college student, have you figured out by now that you have everything inside of you to complete your journey?

If you have gotten to this point in the book, it tells me that you have some academic goals you would like to accomplish, and that you are serious about your destiny. It's time to take charge of what is important, and there is no better way to do this except to start. Below, I have created a list of final things you should know.

Things to know:

- ✓ It is never too late to start.
- ✓ Preparation matters in the end though it may seem difficult in the beginning.
- ✓ The first draft of your essay will not be the way you envisioned it, but it's called a draft for a reason.
- ✓ You are not alone. There are plenty of people in your shoes.
- ✓ Develop an academic plan and know that it may change overtime.
- ✓ Research the field you're entering.
- ✓ Co-op work experience: If you have to work while going to school, why not get credit for it that will apply to your elective units for graduation. Each school is different, but worth the effort to research.
- ✓ Teachers and staff have gone through the process. Do not be afraid to ask them for assistance.
- ✓ Everyone's story is different. Do not be afraid to tell yours.
- ✓ There are certain programs specifically designed to help you apply for colleges. Seek them.
- ✓ The English department of your school should be able to help you with your essay, or point you in the right direction.
- ✓ Scholarship committees want to help fund your education. It is up to you to go after it.

Motivation Corner

Tenacity to Push Forward

I ended my high school commencement speech with this Anatole France quote: "To accomplish great things, we must not only act, but also dream; not only plan, but also believe." This quote has remained a constant and is a prelude for all facets of my life. I graduated with my Bachelors of Arts in Psychology from East Carolina University. There was tremendous pressure being the first grandchild on both sides of my family to attend college. I can now say that the pressure was heightened by my own expectations and standards of myself. It is very easy to become your own worst enemy to the point of exhaustion, burnout, and fatigue. I changed majors twice and often worried that I was a disappointment. Growing up I had this vision of what my life should be and when it wasn't turning out that way I didn't know how to cope. I put myself in a miserable glass house for years full of self-doubt, weight gain, and depression. Constantly being bogged down by worry and drama clouds our minds and feeds the ego. I am super thankful that presently this house has been renovated with proper insulation. I will never forget walking across the stage and hugging my dad, the release I felt was exhilarating. I call that release the "new journey" release. We shouldn't wait for a huge life-changing event to feel refreshed. Every day is a new journey and we must treat it as such. Years later I am aware that I am fine just as I am, and I can make it through. I have learned that I can make my family and others around me proud by simply being the individual that God has called me to be.

    I was 90lbs heavier during my freshman and sophomore years of college. During my junior and senior years I made the decision to lose the weight. I successfully lost around 30lbs during that time, but unfortunately it wasn't the healthy way and I gained it right back. I have now lost and kept off those 90lbs for the past two years the healthy way, even with a busy schedule. I am so thankful that I showcased my journey through my YouTube series where I have inspired hundreds and maybe thousands to become a healthier version of themselves. You can lose and or maintain your weight while balancing your life. Life is all about balance and you can truly do anything you put your mind to. I am a true testament of that statement. As I continue to progress I want to challenge even more people especially young adults to take control of their health the right way. I also want to encourage others to love and value themselves on the inside and out. I absolutely love my brand MissPtv and I will continue to produce content that promotes inspiration, motivation, and fun along the way.

    I discovered so much about myself while furthering my education. I discovered that knowledge is power! That power will never be stolen from you. I have discovered the key to unleash my power is helping others to become the greatest version of themselves. Never would I have imagined that I would be entertaining thousands on a weekly basis by hosting my own web series. I would have never thought this route were possible had it not been for my education. The tools that were given to me throughout my collegiate career can never be replaced. This web series has turned into a brand where I am able to consult, train, and transform lives on a daily basis. Obtaining a degree has to be one of the most rewarding accomplishments in my life. I not only made my family proud but also myself. Without my education I wouldn't have the knowledge, the confidence, and the tenacity to push forward through circumstances that may come my way. The doors that continue to open are truly a testament to hard work and determination. I encourage you to change your perspective and value your mind. You can accomplish great things! Dreams can come to fruition with planning, action, and strong belief.

Tara Powell received her Bachelors of Arts in Psychology from East Carolina University. She is a self-motivator, entrepreneur and coach. Her current and future goals are to expand her coaching services to encourage and inspire individuals with their weight goals, and self-worth.
She currently resides in Fayetteville, North Carolina with her family.

Additional Tips

Additional Tip #1: *Scholarship Thief* –Do not just take the money and run. Always send a thank you note over the course of your academics so they'll know how you're doing.

Additional Tip #2: Never send your personal information to an unknown illegitimate scholarship, especially online. It is best to check with your local scholarship office so that you can feel comfortable in applying.

Additional Tip #3: If a scholarship asks you for money/entrance fee to apply, avoid it. You are trying to get money, not give it away.

Additional Tip #4: Moral support from family and friends are important.

Additional Tip #5: Remember, it's possible to avoid school loans and get through college debt free. Some people just sign on the dotted line because they do not want to do the leg work to get scholarships. I avoided loans because I still desired to purchase a home one day, buy a car, work on establishing better and good credit, and invest into my future. Do the work, and watch it happen for you.

Additional Tip #6: Mediocre grades are an obstacle, but challenge is your middle name. You have what it takes.

Additional Tip #7: Counselors are there to help. If for some reason you feel different, speak to their boss, or another counselor in the office.

Additional Tip #8: This is a process and it does not happen overnight.

Additional Tip #9: Interviews for scholarships: What is your mission statement? Figure out your goal in life beforehand.

Additional Tip #10: Convert Challenges into Opportunities. Never let an obstacle decide your outcome.

Additional Tip #11: Research the committee that will be reviewing your application. Believe me, it matters.

Additional Tip #12: Know the names of the staff in the financial aid/scholarship office. You'll be the first they think of when opportunities come along.

Additional Tip #13: Online Donations such as GoFund Me are good ways to raise money. Please research because most of them charge a fee.

Additional Tip #14: Possible internships and/or Community service looks good on your academic résumé. If you have not committed to any of these, try starting now. Your local church is a good place to start.

Additional Tip #15: When requesting transcripts, remember to order multiple copies because they will be needed during this process.

Additional Tip #16: Financial Breakdown –Know how much your academics will cost all the way from tuition to transportation to food and clothes. You do not want any unnecessary fees showing up at the last minute.

Additional Tip #17: Direct Deposit is your friend! Avoid getting checks mailed to you, as there can be delays.

Additional Tip #18: Pay attention to disbursement dates, and make sure that they align with your fee deadlines.

Additional Tip #19: Break up the process of applying to school and scholarships in sections. The last thing you need on your plate is the feeling of being overwhelmed.

Additional Tip #20: Start as early as possible, and be prepared to show up for yourself before anyone else does.

Additional Tip #21: Jot down notes when you do not understand something so that you can ask your counselor, mentor or advisor during your meeting.

Additional Tip #22: Deadlines are important! Keep track of everything you do so that you will not miss out.

Note:
Send me an email if you find other useful resources not listed here to be included in the next book, or addressed online. Subject to further research.

*"I am not as strong as I thought I was.
I am stronger!"*

Last Minute Check List

Here is a quick last minute list to check off some of the things needed to be successful during the process. Remember, you can add more to the list as needed, but I have started it for you. Have you completed these?

- FAFSA ☐
- Submitting Application by due date ☐
- 2-3 Professional Recommendations ☐
- Scholarship Essay/Cover Letter ☐
- University Application Essay (If needed) ☐
- Résumé ☐
- Official Transcripts (Some will take unofficial) ☐
- Estimated Tuition Breakdown ☐
- Other possible Expenses ☐
- Interview Preparation ☐
- Consulting with your Counselor ☐
- Thank you Letters ☐
- _____ ☐
- _____ ☐
- _____ ☐
- _____ ☐
- _____ ☐

Congratulations

"The most successful person isn't the best in the room, nor the most popular student on campus, neither the most talented person around. The most successful person is the one who works the hardest, endures through the strongest failures, and overcomes the highest mountain."

Throughout my academic career I would go online or to my scholarship office and look at some acceptance letters. This was an opportunity for me to begin seeing myself receiving one of them. I would look at these letters and picture myself being handed one by the faculty of the school. Envisioning yourself winning will be a major part in how you receive. Sometimes it will take you going to the scholarship office to look at someone else's achievements, or speaking with friends who have been down the path you are on. If you can see yourself receiving, then it is absolutely possible to obtain it.

I will never forget when I won my first scholarship. I was attending my local community college, and was nearing the end of my term. During the course of the school year, I would search out scholarships and apply to them in hopes that I would be the recipient. I did not have a 4.0 so it was a bit intimidating at first, but I was determined. I remember working hard writing essays, speaking with my counselors, dropping in to the scholarship office, and completing applications before going to class. For this particular scholarship I had done all that I could so there was nothing left to do but wait. The day that I received the scholarship I was attending the Career Development Program. It was on a Saturday afternoon and I had just gotten off of work. I walked into the room and sat down in my seat like I usually do. As soon as I got comfortable, one of the instructors, Reginald Turner, said to the class, "I would like to take this time to congratulate Toi for winning the Kennedy King Memorial Scholarship". It was a surreal moment because everyone began clapping but I could not say a word. I ran out of the room down the hallway to the scholarship office and met Claudia Acevedo there and she confirmed it for me. I was ecstatic.

The point I am trying to make is that if you do the work, write the essay, meet with your counselor and position yourself, you are creating room to receive. All the hard work in applying for multiple scholarships was now paying off, and I immediately started to get more congratulation letters in the mail. I had won and that was a good feeling all in itself. There may be times when you feel discouraged, but I am here to tell you that you will get back what you put in. Lean on your professors and counselors for assistance while going through the process. It is okay to not know which way to go because soon you will discover the right path to take.

Remember, when it's time to graduate, and you've completed all of your tasks, there are certain fees you must pay for your degree which includes but not limited to:

1. Graduation Application Fee
2. Cap and Gown Fee
3. Graduation Commencement Fee
4. Official Transcripts (Most colleges, the first two are free).

These are the main fees due before you can actually receive your degree. Other fees may be added as necessary, depending on the college/university you attend.

Congratulations are now in order. You have made the first step in receiving scholarships and finishing your degree. Keep going!

Starter Essay Questions

1. What value will you bring to the school and/or major department?
2. What sets you apart from other applicants?
3. What organizations are you part of, or would like to be part of?
4. What are your degree expectations?
5. What prior accomplishments have you completed in the last three years?
6. What year do you expect to graduate?
7. What is your major and why did you choose it?
8. What school are you attending/or have applied for? Why did you choose this school?
9. Describe a class or teacher who have impacted your education?
10. How has an adversity or challenge in your life influenced your education?
11. What do you plan to do with your degree upon graduation?
12. If you could change one thing in your community, what would it be? Why?
13. What does education mean to you? Be specific. Be unique.
14. What one challenge in your life taught you the value of patience?
15. What is your family background? How has it influenced you?
16. Have you completed any community service? Explain.
17. How have you grown in the last four years? Explain.
18. When is your start date to attend college?
19. Do you expect to graduate with your class? If not, explain the setbacks you anticipate happening?
20. What is your support system like? Do you have positive influences around to support your desire for education? If not, why?

FAQ'S Answered

Q. I have never applied for scholarships before –can you point me in the right direction on where to start?
A. If you are a high school student, your counselor should be the first contact. If you have already enrolled in college, immediately go to your campus scholarship office for further assistance.

Q. How many classes should I take to qualify for scholarships?
A. Most scholarships require full-time status with at least 12 units or more. Depending on the scholarship, you may need to refer to the specific bulletin for further information.

Q. How are scholarships issued?
A. Scholarships are mostly issued to the school you are attending. Once your fees and tuition have been paid, the college or university will either mail you a check or deposit the remaining amount into your account you have listed, so make sure your account information is accurate.

Q. My grades are not that good. Can I still apply for scholarships?
A. Yes. Make sure that you apply for the scholarships that are financial need base. The selection committee will consider your application based on need, not merit. My advice is to continue working on your grades to make them better, and write one amazing essay.

Q. What if I receive a scholarship, but have to take a semester off for personal reasons?
A. Make sure you speak with your counselor and the financial aid office to document your leave. Also, contact the issuing scholarship committee, and speak with them regarding your situation. If you wish to keep your scholarship upon returning to school, communication is key.

Q. What is the maximum amount of money I can receive per academic year?

A. It all depends on the tuition cost of your particular school. For complete and accurate information, please go to your financial aid office and speak with a counselor.

Q. Can I use the same essay for multiple scholarships?

A. Yes. The majority of scholarship essay questions are the same. Depending on the type of scholarship and questions asked, you may need to edit accordingly.

Q. I am finding it difficult to write my scholarship essay. Can you give me some pointers?

A. Please refer to the essay section in this book (page 40). This section includes starter questions to help you begin your essay. Also, refer to the specific scholarship you're applying for. They will provide you with the necessary questions. I have also listed a "starter essay question" section for your convenience (page 124).

If you have more questions that are not listed, email me at dreamloudinc@yahoo.com with your question. It will be answered to the best of my knowledge.

Author's Bio

A native of Los Angeles, California, *Toi Nichelle* began her career on a road that is rare amongst her peers. Having gone through challenges some would deem as traumatizing such as homelessness, abuse, neglect and suicidal attempts, she has cleared herself from the gates of low self-esteem to a balance of favor through faith. *"You can obtain the desires of your heart with a little hard work, sweat, patience and by not being afraid to fall when everyone is looking,"* she says when confronted with questions from those seeking advice.

It is not easy. As a matter of fact you will come up against mountains which will make your dreams seem far beyond reach, but a leading example of perseverance is seen through *Toi Nichelle's* struggle. Within the last five years she has come from homelessness and mind-boggling low self-esteem. These situations gave her a reason to fight and run towards her destiny with no intent on giving up.

In 2007, she established Dream Loud Ink Publishing, which is in transition to publish material to heal our communities, and The Hush Language: A Young Girl's Breakthrough where she helps to encourage teens who struggle with abuse to move forward.

Toi Nichelle is a recipient of numerous scholarships some including, Kennedy King Scholarship, David Schirra Memorial Scholarship, Los Medanos Fund Scholarship and the Gilman Study Abroad Scholarship. She recently studied at the University of East Anglia in Norwich, England for an academic year, while touring through Europe to places like Paris, Italy and Amsterdam. *Toi Nichelle* has received her A.A. in Liberal Arts and Humanities from Los Medanos College (2011), and a B.A. in English: Creative Writing from San Francisco State University (2013).

Her professional goals include, developing as a business professional to be well equipped in all facets of life, and assisting with raising money to distribute scholarships to students of various ages through her scholarship foundation, *The Scholarship Thief*; strengthening her social skills as an individual by connecting with like-minded people who are seeking to improve their personal standards of life; evolve as an inspirational speaker and writer to be the voice for so many young girls and boys who are silenced because of their childhood, ultimately helping them to find their way; and continuing to become a better person who fights with both fists.

The Scholarship Thief is her third book in print. *Toi Nichelle* currently resides in East Bay, California where she is surrounded by awesome friends and a powerful God.

Scholarship Resource Alphabetical Listing

Although there are thousands of scholarship websites, here are some resources for scholarships to help you start. I am in no way endorsing these sites, but have used some of them during my scholarship search, and personally know others who have as well. Also, make sure you check the campus scholarship bulletin by your selected university. You can do this by going to the scholarship or financial aid office.

A

AAC'S Behavioral Health Academic Scholarship
http://www.aplaceformom.com/scholarship

Abbott and Fenner Scholarship
http://www.abbottandfenner.com/scholarships.htm

Absolute Dental Scholarship
http://www.absolutedental.com/dentists-scholarship-program/

The AccuLynx Scholarship for Higher Education
http://www.acculynx.com/scholarship

ACS Scholarship Seed Program
http://www.acs.org/content/acs/en/funding-and-awards/scholarships/projectseed.html

American Business Women's Association
http://www.abwa-pathfinder.org/scholarships.htm

Anita Borg Memorial Scholarship
http://www.boomtownig.com/about/scholarship/

Annual Creative Scholarship Award
http://www.858graphics.com/creative_scholarship_program.html

Artistic Excellence in Print Design & Marketing Scholarship
http://www.printaholic.com/scholarship/

Arts Recognition and Talent Search Sponsored by the White House
http://www.youngarts.org/us-presidential-scholars-arts

Aspiring Fashion Professional Scholarship
http://www.fashion-schools.org/aspiring-fashion-professional-scholarship-program

AXA Achievement Scholarship
http://www.axa.scholarshipamerica.org/

B

Bank of America Student Leaders Internship
www.bankofamerica.com/studentleaders

Big Future
www.bigfuture.collegeboard.org

Blackhawk Women's Scholarship Fund
http://bwscholarshipfund.com/scholarships.htm

Boomtown Internet Group Scholarship Opportunity
http://www.boomtownig.com/about/scholarship/

Boren Scholarship (study abroad)
www.borenawards.org

Brick House Security College Scholarship
http://www.brickhousesecurity.com/category/company+info/scholarship.do

Burger King Scholars
www.scholarshipamerica.org/burgerkingscholars/

C

California Student Aid Commission
www.csac.ca.gov/

Casey Family Program for Students from Foster Care
http://www.fc2success.org/programs/scholarships-and-grants/

Chegg Scholarship
http://www.chegg.com/scholarships/chegg-monthly-scholarship-october-2015

Clark Scholarship
https://www.gemsociety.org/scholarships/

Coca-Cola Foundation
www.cocacolascholarsfoundation.org/

College Bound Brotherhood Scholarship
https://app.smarterselect.com/programs/25909-Marcus-Foster-Education-Fund

CrossLites Scholarship
http://www.crosslites.com/about-the-contest/

D

72 Degrees National Scholarship
http://72degreesaz.com/72-degrees-national-scholarship/

Douglas W. Robinson Student Success Scholarship (CSULB)
https://web.csulb.edu/divisions/students/scholarships/search/display.php?sID=1343

Dream Deferred Essay Contest Scholarship
http://www.hamsaweb.org/essay/

TheDream.US Scholarship
http://www.thedream.us/scholars/

E

East Bay College Fund
www.eastbaycollegefund.org

Educational Advancement Foundation, Inc.
http://www.akaeaf.org/undergraduate_scholarships.htm

Emily M. Hewitt Memorial Scholarship
http://bigtrees.org/events-programs/scholarship-fund/

Equality Scholarships
www.equalityscholarship.org

F

Fast Web Scholarship Site
www.fastweb.com

Financial Aid Site
www.finaid.org

Freedom Writers Scholarship Foundation
http://www.freedomwritersfoundation.org/fw-scholars

G

The Gates Millennium Scholars Program
http://www.gmsp.org/default.aspx

Gilman (study abroad)
www.iie.org

Gladys A. Moreau Scholarship Award (Los Angeles)
http://wit-la.org/scholarship_moreau.asp

Goedeker's College Scholarship
http://www.goedekers.com/college-scholarship

Golden Women Scholarship
http://www.goldenwomen.org/home/scholarships

H Hardy Wolf and Downing
http://www.acwa.com/content/acwa-water-law-policy-scholarship

The Harry S. Truman Scholarship Foundation
http://www.truman.gov/

Honors Graduation Multi-Media Scholarship
https://www.honorsgraduation.com/graduation-scholarship.htm

Hotels Cheap Scholarships
http://www.hotelscheap.org/scholarship

I Innovation in Education Scholarship
https://web.csulb.edu/divisions/students/scholarships/search/display.php?sID=1485

J The Jackie Robinson Foundation
http://www.jackierobinson.org/about/programs.php

John and Flora Olsen Scholarship (CSULB)
https://web.csulb.edu/divisions/students/scholarships/search/display.php?sID=1251

K Kennedy King (Bay Area)
www.kennedyking.org

The Christopher W. Keyser Undergraduate Scholarship
http://www.keyserdefense.com/contact-us/christopher-keyser-scholarship

L

LAGRANT Foundation (TLF)
http://www.lagrantfoundation.org/

Learning Path Student Scholarships
http://learningpath.org/articles/learningpathorg_college_scholarship_program.html

Lemberg Law Lemon Justice Scholarship
http://www.lemonjustice.com/i/1000-lemberg-law-lemon-justice-scholarship/

The Levin Firm Scholarship
http://www.levininjuryfirm.com/scholarship/

The Levy Production Group's "Rising Star in Production" Scholarship
http://www.levyproductiongroup.com/video-production-scholarship/

Live Your Dream Awards –Soroptimist International of the Americas
http://www.soroptimist.org/awards/apply.html

M

Making Waves Foundation's Bay Area College & Alumni Program & Scholarship
http://www.making-waves.org/programs/education/college/capbayarea

Marin Education Fund
http://www.10000degrees.org/students/scholarships/

Charles Moo Scholarship
http://www.10000degrees.org/students/scholarships/

My Visa Source Scholarship
http://www.myvisasource.com/1000-annual-scholarship-from-my-visa-source

N

Navolutions Scholarship
http://www.navolutions.com/scholarships/

New Leader Scholarship
http://www.navolutions.com/scholarships/

NFIB Young Entrepreneur Award
www.NFIB.com/YEA

O

Oakland Dollars for Scholars
http://www.navolutions.com/scholarships/

P

The Ron Paul Scholarships
http://www.navolutions.com/scholarships/

Penn Lease Transportation Scholarship
http://www.pennlease.com/company-profile/penn-lease-scholarship-20152016-school-year/

Q

QuikShip Toner Scholarship
http://www.quikshiptoner.com/catalog/scholarship_program.php

R

Reagan Foundation Scholarship
http://www.reaganfoundation.org/GE-RFScholarships.aspx

Ron Brown Scholar Program
https://www.ronbrown.org/

Ronald McDonald House Charities
http://www.rmhc.org/rmhc-us-scholarships

S

Scholarship Search Site
www.scholarships.com

Scholarship Search Site
www.scholarshiplibrary.com

Stephen J. Brady Stop Hunger Scholarship
http://www.sodexofoundation.org/hunger_us/scholarships/scholarships.asp

Students Rising Above Program
http://studentsrisingabove.org/

T

Thurgood Marshall College Fund Scholarships
http://tmcf.org/our-scholarships/current-scholarships

Tony Ferris Memorial Scholarship (CSULB)
https://web.csulb.edu/divisions/students/scholarships/search/display.php?sID=645

U

Union Plus Education Foundation
https://www.unionplus.org/college-education-financing/union-plus-scholarship#amount

United Negro College Fund
www.uncf.org

W

Walmart Foundation
https://walmart.scholarsapply.org/associate/

Women & Philanthropy Reentry Scholarship (CSULB)
https://web.csulb.edu/divisions/students/scholarships/search/display.php?sID=567

Y

Young Arts Foundation
http://www.youngarts.org/apply

Your Local Security Scholarship
http://yourlocalsecurity.com/scholarship

Contact

For bookings or to request Author Toi Nichelle for speaking engagements with youth and young adult groups and school assemblies please contact:

Mailing Address:
Dream Loud Ink, Publishing
C/O Toi Nichelle
PO BOX 3411
Antioch, Ca 94509

Email:

spirituallyunique@yahoo.com
dreamloudinc@yahoo.com

www.ingramcontent.com/pod-product-compliance
Lightning Source LLC
Chambersburg PA
CBHW071224090426
42736CB00014B/2960